Celebrating 50 years of service

1962 - 2012

McMillan
HOTELS

McMillan

THE COUPLE WHO BUILT
THE FAMILY BUSINESS

A DOCUMENTARY BY
MICHAEL MARSHALL

'Do you think we've done the right thing, opening a hotel?'
Hammy McMillan in 1962, six months after purchasing North West Castle, Stranraer

McMillan - The Couple Who Built the Family Business

First published in 2012 by
Breathing Space Productions

ISBN   978 0 9565894 2 2

British Library Cataloguing-in-Publication Data
A catalogue record for this book is available from The British Library

McMillan *THE COUPLE WHO BUILT THE FAMILY BUSINESS*

Contents

The book you are about to read is the journey of a lifetime -
one that over the past six months I've been priviliged to
share, meeting the McMillan family and talking with them
at great length about their hotel enterprise, founded in 1962
and which now deservedly celebrates its Golden Jubilee.
Alongside the family, I've also been able to meet and observe
many members of the hotel teams at work. Their valued
contributions and the recollections of those who were once
part of the family of workers are greatly appreciated.

Special thanks must go to Fiona Hardie who, as the
McMillan family archivist, has helped me enormously with
the task of tracking down pictures, press cuttings and items
of memorabilia that all help to tell this story; to everyone
in the McMillan family - they have been a source of much
encouragement, providing additional material, memorabilia,
and guidance - reading, checking and double-checking
manuscripts. Their friendship and hospitality at home in
every sense matches the welcomes they extend at their hotels.

Finally, to my wife Jean for her enthusiastic and patient
support throughout this project.

Michael Marshall

Meet the Family!

David Hardie   Lorna McMillan   Susy McMillan   Graham Cowan

Fiona Hardie   Hamilton McMillan   Douglas McMillan   Fay Cowan   John Munro

Hammy McMillan   Janet McMillan   Gail Munro

STRANRAER FROM SOUTH.

1 - Prologue

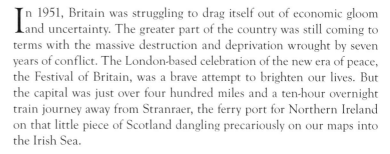

In 1951, Britain was struggling to drag itself out of economic gloom and uncertainty. The greater part of the country was still coming to terms with the massive destruction and deprivation wrought by seven years of conflict. The London-based celebration of the new era of peace, the Festival of Britain, was a brave attempt to brighten our lives. But the capital was just over four hundred miles and a ten-hour overnight train journey away from Stranraer, the ferry port for Northern Ireland on that little piece of Scotland dangling precariously on our maps into the Irish Sea.

It might just as well have been three thousand miles away for one twenty-year old lad, born in this south-western outpost of Bonnie Galloway in 1931. After completing an apprenticeship with a local builder, and encouraged by his parents, Hamilton Coats McMillan, the third of six sons, boarded the train to London, and then on to Southampton, where a ship would take him to join relatives in Canada.

Hammy, as he was known to everyone around him, had embarked on his great adventure; a replay of what had, and still happens for many thousands of Scots who leave these shores to seek their fortunes.

That might have been the end of the story for us here in Scotland, were it not for the chance reading of a report a few years later in a local Wigtownshire newspaper.

Hammy's bold vision and the unstinting help of his equally enthusiastic wife Janet created the perfect recipe for something exciting to happen. Now, half a century later, and with a full supporting cast of five children, the name McMillan has become synonymous with pride and excellence in Scotland's hospitality industry. From builder of houses to architect of an award-winning hotel group is an epic in itself. But Hammy's story is also about those who've played a part in this success – in particular his family, the loyal hotel teams and countless travellers that have signed the guest registers.

For Hammy - the man who built a business – the timeless Gaelic greeting 'Ceud Mìle Fàilte' – a hundred thousand welcomes – means just that.

2 · Before It All Began

Travellers, usually weary and frustrated by the final hundred miles or so of the twisting and frequently intimidating A75 Euroroute that links Britain's motorway network to the port of Stranraer, have been greatly relieved to find rest and relaxation at the historic landmark and hotel that is the North West Castle. Approaching this gleaming white, somewhat colonial and tropical-looking establishment, it's the welcome that is equally impressive. Not just from the staff, but also its owner. Hammy McMillan's stamp on this place is unforgettable, especially to the first-time visitor. More often than not, no sooner had you arrived than Hammy would appear at your side, greet you, and with your bags under his command whisk you off to a comfortable room. Above all, he has that most essential requirement of anyone involved in the hotel industry – the ability to remember a name, and link it with a face – even after a gap of a year or so. Formidable indeed.

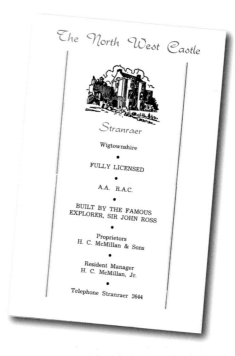

The North West Castle

Stranraer

Wigtownshire
•
FULLY LICENSED
•
A.A.   R.A.C.
•
BUILT BY THE FAMOUS
EXPLORER, SIR JOHN ROSS
•
Proprietors
H. C. McMillan & Sons
•
Resident Manager
H. C. McMillan, Jr.
•
Telephone Stranraer 2644

Hammy McMillan is no stranger to work. The McMillan family have embraced the ethic for four generations now. At the time when Queen Victoria was celebrating her Diamond Jubilee, Hammy's grandfathers were building houses and repairing roads. In the depression years of the 1920's, his father would be working as a porter at the harbour, busy with passengers arriving by train from London or Glasgow to catch the ferry to Northern Ireland. As a young boy, Hammy remembers the railway line and the Harbour station that would stable the London-bound train, affectionately known as 'The Paddy', but officially known as *The Northern Irishman*, sometimes with as many as seventeen coaches. Two steam engines would be needed to haul it overnight up steep inclines and over majestic viaducts on a route long since disappeared.

The early McMillan dynasty -

top: Hammy's great-grandfather: Alexander.

right to left:

Grandparents: Andrew & Elizabeth McCandlish (Lizzie).
Parents: Hamilton Coats & Margaret Campbell (Maggie).

left: Hammy in 1933, then aged 15 months, with his two older brothers Andrew and William.

Agnew Crescent, Stranraer

The McMillan's first home was in Agnew Crescent. In the nineteen thirties this part of Stranraer was called the Clayhole. At No. 30 they had two rooms and shared a toilet with two other families. From here, 'Wee Hammy', as he was known to his grandparents, would walk along the shore of Loch Ryan to Kirkcolm village where a warm welcome was always waiting for him.

Town life in Stranraer was much the same as anywhere else for someone growing up – apart from school and the church, there were the distractions of the shops and the weekly cattle market and, in the centre of it all, the imposing and forbidding Castle of St John. A fortified house; a court; a prison and even a military garrison at the time of the Covenanters, a young imagination could run riot around here.

NORTH WEST CASTLE STRANRAER

There was a chance for an even greater sense of adventure just down by the shore. Looking out across Loch Ryan was the castellated four-storey North West Castle. Surrounded by high walls, with a lodge and boathouse, it was built in 1819 by the Arctic explorer Rear Admiral Sir John Ross. He had not long returned from an expedition to seek the North West Passage – the sea route linking the Atlantic and Pacific Oceans – the hunt for which had excited explorers for centuries. In this mission he had been accompanied by his nephew, James Clark Ross, also from Stranraer, and who on a later expedition also discovered the magnetic North Pole.

North West Castle

opposite:

Rear Admiral Sir John Ross - portrait by Benjamin Rawlinson Faulkner. (National Galleries of Scotland)

The view from the Residents' Lounge at North West Castle.

Sir John was a keen naturalist, and inside the outer walls of North West Castle a great garden flourished. A glass-covered porch was built to house a eucalyptus tree, while elsewhere in the garden there was a fig tree brought from St Helena at the time of Napoleon's imprisonment on the island. His passion for the sea and the far north was reflected in the interiors of the house. Along with a private chapel, there was a small theatre with scenic displays of snowy wastes, seals and polar bears. Inside the house he built a replica of his cabin on the *Victory*, one of the ships that he used for the perilous Arctic voyages. Here he would entertain guests with demonstrations on polar navigation.

So the North West Castle already held much in store for young Hammy, perhaps more than he could ever have dreamed possible. The house was then in the ownership of the Cunningham family, one of their number a respected pioneer in education. But in 1941, it was taken over by the Royal Air Force to be used as its headquarters in the area. Loch Ryan had become a top secret site for the development of the Mulberry Harbours, the floating installations that would be used in the D-Day landings of 1944. Not that the military presence was any deterrent to Hammy:

"I remember when I was a youngster, about 11 or 12, I used to go into the garden of the North West Castle and help myself to apples. I got into serious trouble once because I went in when the October Carnival was in town, there were two or three of us, and we got the apples. We started selling them at the Show. It wasn't long before word got back to my father, and I fairly got kicked up the road."

Apart from the comings and goings of the harbour, Stranraer and the surrounding countryside of the Rhins peninsula is the province of highly productive dairy farms. Galloway's reputation for fine cheese making grew when the first modern creamery was opened in the town in 1899.

Just up the road, a mile or so out of Stranraer, at Auchtralure, the view over the town and harbour and Loch Ryan is breathtaking. In the distance, Ailsa Craig – the grey, granite dome that is home to thousands of seabirds and at one time the main source for just as many Scottish curling stones.

The farm at Auchtralure was typical of many family enterprises. Occasionally, Hammy would go there to thin turnips for the owner, John Dalrymple. The Dalrymples had five children – including Janet, the girl who would one day marry Hammy. Today she vividly recalls the daily pattern of work when she wasn't attending school at the Stranraer Academy:

"It wasn't a huge farm, but there were quite a lot of people working there – there was a ploughman, a dairyman, and there were always extra hands to help out. The milk went into churns and these were picked up by lorry from the nearby creamery. On the rare occasions when there had been a heavy snowfall we had to transport the milk ourselves. The everyday life of the farm would always be the topic of conversation – the crops, the market, the weather."

In those days the great majority of cattle were the traditional Ayrshire breed – rich red-brown and white, and with horns:

"Milking, although I never had to do any of it, was done in the byre. At harvest time however we all worked – I drove the tractor on the farm, but I wasn't old enough to drive on the roads then. I helped look after the hens - my daily task was searching and gathering in the eggs which we used in the house. Many of them would be used by my mother for her huge baking sessions. I learned many of my cooking skills at the farmhouse table."

Summer skies near the Rhins of Galloway

**Sheuchan Primary School,
Stranraer**
*Hammy, 11 years old, is fourth
from the left in the back row.*

Back at Agnew Crescent, Hammy's teenage years beckoned:

"In my mid-teens, I thought a lot about what I should be doing with myself. What trade to follow? I left school at fourteen and I started an apprenticeship in the building trade in the town, starting work with my grandfather. That didn't last very long however as my uncle took over the business, and I just didn't get on with him. There was a firm from Lanarkshire building houses on the Sheuchan Parks Estate in Stranraer at the time. So I went along to see them and got a job as an apprentice joiner. I was lucky to get in with a good firm."

Those who knew Hammy in those early work days recall how he was a model apprentice, and was often cited as an example to new recruits.

The McMillan family at home -

now living at Parklea Gardens, this picture is from the late 1940's. Hammy (left) is with his brother Andrew, his father and mother; brother Billy, and below, his younger brothers John and James.

The many branches of the McMillan family had become somewhat scattered. His maternal Aunt Belle and her husband had left Scotland and started a new life in Canada before the First World War. This was indeed the land of promise, and their persuasive letters home soon began to appeal to Hammy:

"They had always wanted some of us to go. And because it was either that or do National Service I decided to go. My brother had just come out of the army having completed his National Service, which he hated, so it was a simple decision to make!"

Hammy's ship docked at Montreal after an uneventful October crossing. He'd come to Canada's largest city, where just a week before, Princess Elizabeth and Prince Philip had arrived to start their visit to this vast, exciting country.

Probably the first thing Hammy would have noticed on disembarking, as he found his way to the main railway station for the next stage of his journey, would have been the almost universal use of French rather than the anticipated English. However, his final destination lay some 560 miles to the south-west in Ontario where his aunt and uncle, Belle and Peter Matthews were waiting to welcome him.

Pleasant Place, in the City of Windsor, lies just a block away from the great St. Lawrence Seaway that divides Canada and the United States. A peaceful, leafy suburb that is in stark contrast to its brash neighbour across the water: Detroit, 'The Motor City'. Hammy settled in quickly with his aunt and uncle and began looking for work. 1951 was a difficult time – the car-making giants Ford, General Motors and Chrysler were relocating their Canadian operations and there was considerable unemployment.

Luckily for Hammy, the Woodall Construction Company, founded by two immigrant brothers in 1909 and which had become a prosperous family business, took him on – in his first year as an apprentice. He was quickly promoted to be a foreman-joiner. The company's projects were frequently large scale affairs – despite the unemployment, Windsor was a growing business centre in the province, with new housing, industrial complexes and prestigious public buildings, providing opportunities for those willing to work.

Hammy was enjoying his new life: while he spent most of his spare time working, he found time to take holidays, crossing into the United States, and driving across the endless prairie lands and up through the Rocky Mountains to the West Coast. After eight years with Woodall Construction, Hammy had acquired enough knowledge and self confidence to go it alone. He set up in partnership with another skilled tradesman, and the Windsor Construction and Home Improvement Company, working mainly on small extensions and home improvements, was established.

Hammy enjoying some relaxation in Ontario

Janet Dalrymple, aged 16

Back home in Stranraer, at Auchtralure Farm, Janet Dalrymple, although some eight years younger than Hammy, was now facing a similar life-shaping decision on choice of career. Leaving school at fifteen, but having to wait until she was seventeen to start training as a nurse, she began looking for work in Stranraer. Her father, John Dalrymple, was convinced that she would never progress to nursing if she followed that route. He insisted that she should stay at home and help on the farm. Besides, her brother, who was some six years older, and working on the farm had decided to emigrate to Australia. With two younger brothers, one of them still an infant, there would be plenty of domestic duties in store!

Unlike the ease and speed with which we can communicate instantly with anyone, anywhere in the world today, it could be a very difficult and expensive affair in the 1950's. In Windsor, Ontario a weekly copy of the *Galloway Advertiser & Wigtown Free Press* would keep Hammy up to date with all the events, gossip and occasional misdeeds of the area. Greatly anticipated air-mail letters would wing their way to and fro across the Atlantic. In Stranraer, an envelope bearing the Windsor postmark would herald news of his activities in Canada – the work, the leisure and the very different weather. But the best news of all would be to read that Hammy was taking a holiday and coming back over to visit.

On one such trip, in February 1956, Hammy was suddenly taken ill with appendicitis. Stranraer's Garrick Hospital, outwardly looking like a large rambling cottage, was where the redundant piece of anatomy was dealt with. In an adjoining ward Janet Dalrymple, now sixteen, had been admitted with the same symptoms, and had undergone a similar visit to the operating theatre.

Recovered from his operation, Hammy prepared to go back to Canada to resume work. But the chance meeting with Janet at the hospital led to the blossoming of an entirely new and prolific stream of transatlantic correspondence.

In 1958, Hammy prepared to welcome her to Canada – she had been allowed by her parents to travel over with an Irish friend of theirs who would act as chaperone. While enjoying a summer holiday touring Canada, on the 11th July they announced their engagement.

Janet returned to Scotland to continue with her nursing training at Seafield Hospital in Ayr. Meanwhile, Hammy progressed with his fast-growing business. After two years he was able to cross the Atlantic once more, this time to claim his young bride.

Married in Ayr in July 1960 and following a honeymoon in the north of Scotland, they both bade their farewells and boarded a BOAC Stratocruiser to fly to Canada. Wedding presents were carefully packed and crated and followed by ship. Janet, now a qualified nurse, anticipated all the excitement of life in a new land:

"Canada was where Hammy's work was and I was more than happy to make that my new home. For a short time we lived in a basement flat in Windsor, while Hammy built a flat above his workshop a short drive away. I got a nursing job and we made a lot of friends while we were there – many of them through Hammy's business and quite a few through my nursing work. We still keep in touch with a lot of people there."

Janet and Hammy on their engagement.

Newspaper Clipping

...LLOWAY ADVERTISER AND WIGTOWNSHIRE FREE...

Council Divided on Acquisition Proposal

North-West Castle as Hotel

NORTH-WEST Castle was a bone of contention at Stranraer Town Council meeting on Monday evening when by ten votes to seven it was agreed not to take any further action regarding its acquisition.

The Castle had been offered to the town for whatever purpose the Council might consider it suitable, but after inspecting it and hearing the views of members and officials, it was agreed not to accept the offer.

Mr R. C. Irving sparked off the discussion by saying that it was with regret he learned of the decision. North-West Castle was one of the town few historical buildings of architectural value. It could be an asset to the town and was wonderfully situated and could be of use to them.

Mrs Brown said she too regretted the decision. She felt it was a very valuable site.

Mrs Murray asked if the Castle had been thoroughly examined and Provost Caughie said it had been examined by their officials.

Mrs Murray: I think we should delay a final decision until we get a report.

Dance Hall and Restaurant

Mr Wm. Hastie said he examined the Castle and was greatly taken on with it. When, however, it was said there was a commercial undertaking interested in it he felt it would be much better to encourage that rather than to take it over. It was in an excellent situation and would make a dance hall with a restaurant above with a tea garden in front. Because of the scarcity of hotel accommodation in the town, however, he felt such a need was paramount. He would not like it for Council offices for the view was so lovely the staff would hardly get any work done for looking at it.

Bailie Brown said he agreed with the description of the site and he understood there was about an acre of ground. He felt the wall could be knocked down and the gardens incorporated into their own gardens to make a wonderful pleasant place. They could have a municipal restaurant with gardens to sit in for the townsfolk. Kilmarnock had taken over such a building and put it to that use.

Development or Hotel

Dean of Guild Martin said he was all in favour of the Council looking into this offer because he felt there would be no one else interested. It would be an asset if it could be incorporated by extension into the present gardens. But as it transpired they were informed there were others interested and having regard to the hotel accommodation situation he felt that was an aspect that they could not afford to overlook. Every encouragement was being given to people to come to Stranraer, but there was no sense in asking people to come when there was no place for them to stay. He felt it would be better to have it developed as an hotel.

Mr J. J. Wales said the Development Association were doing all they could to encourage visitors and they agreed with Mr Martin there was not much sense asking them to come when there was no place for them to stay. He understood there were people interested in it for an hotel.

On a division, ten members voted for the minute and seven for the amendment that the offer should be reconsidered.

Towards the end of June 1961 the usual weekly copy of the *Free Press* arrived in the mail box outside Hammy and Janet's flat. One article in particular caught Hammy's eye. The local Council had been considering the future of North West Castle. The Cunningham family, descendants of its original owner, Sir John Ross, had offered it to the Council for whatever purpose it might deem appropriate. The Council were split on the issue as to what should happen with the historic and architecturally important building. In the end the decision not to take it over was carried by three votes.

Hammy thought this was an opportunity not to be missed, and talked it over at great length with Janet. North West Castle could make an excellent hotel, and Janet was equally enthused:

"In Stranraer in the years before Hammy and I were married, there was the old King's Arms Hotel, which was probably the biggest in the town. It had a super ballroom, but then it was sold, and it was demolished. The site was then redeveloped for the former Woolworth's store. Then there was the George Hotel, the Buck's Head and the Royal Hotel. On one or two occasions while we were in Canada we did say that one day we might go back home and open a pub, although neither of us had ever been to one. Pubs were for one thing in those days."

Time was of the essence – in the sixties a transatlantic telephone call was extremely expensive and had to be booked in advance. Eventually, Hammy got through to his father:

"He asked me if I was interested in North West Castle. Canada was an exciting place to be, but the challenge of beginning something like this was too good to miss. 'Yes', I confirmed. 'Then we'll buy it' my father replied. So Janet and I decided to sell up and come home. That was also the time when Janet's mother and father were visiting us in Canada. They were delighted when they heard our decision and that they would be having us near to them once more. It wasn't all plain sailing though – Janet had to persuade her parents that this was what we really wanted to do. They were not at all keen on us being hoteliers, in fact they were very much against it. But we wanted to do this. We did not want to be swayed."

In July 1961, the family firm of H.C. McMillan and Sons, with a successful grocery business in Glebe Street, purchased North West Castle.

At a quayside in Montreal harbour, the ship's doctor on board the Donaldson Line freighter *Laurentia*, due to sail on October 10th 1961 for Greenock, Scotland, was concerned to find that one of the fifty passengers on board was some seven months pregnant.

He was somewhat anxious that midwifery on the high seas might not be his particular speciality. He need not have worried – Janet McMillan's determination that her first born should be truly Scottish, rather than belonging 'on the high seas', prevailed.

North Rhins landfall

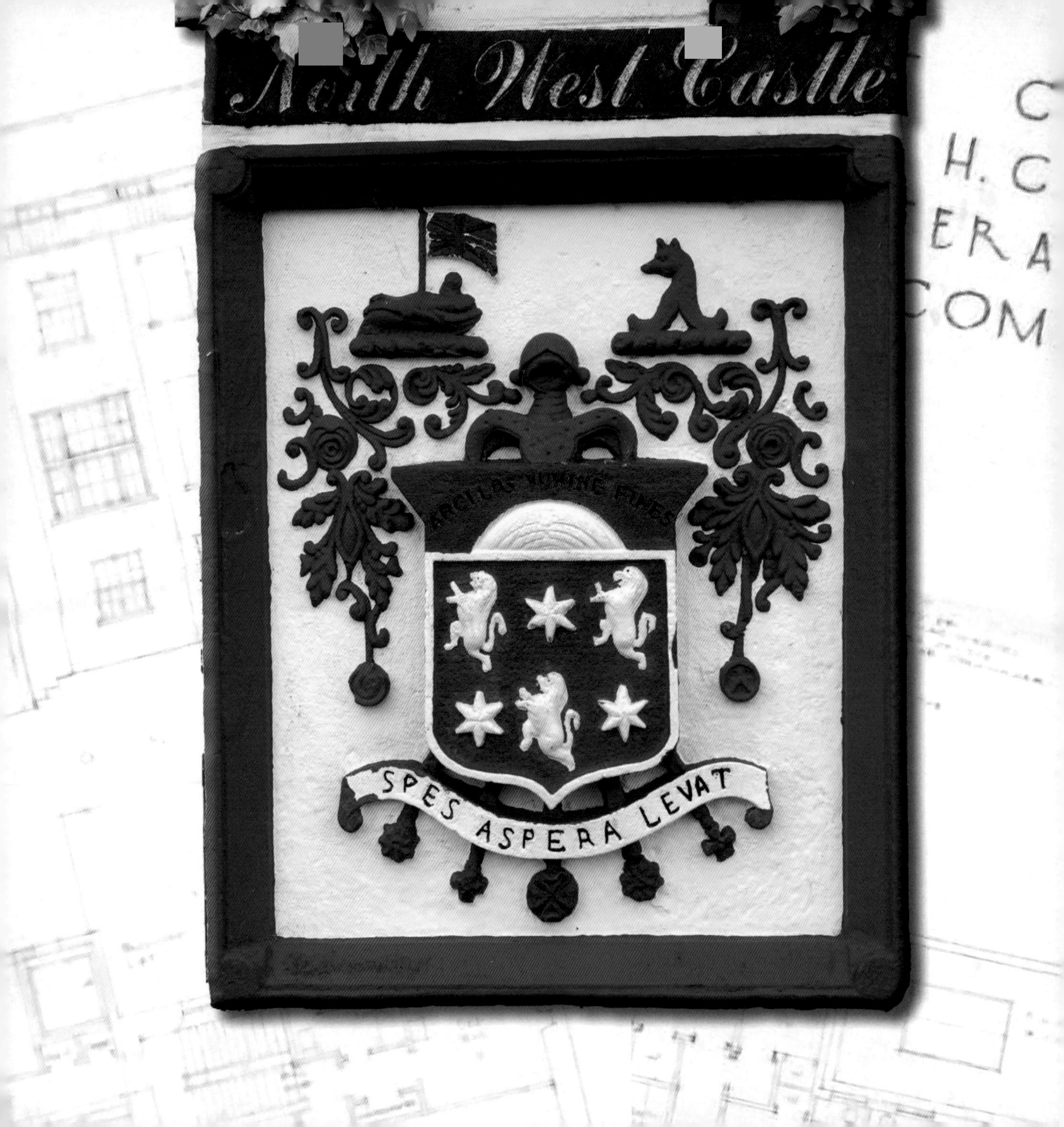
North West Castle
SPES ASPERA LEVAT

3 – Restoration, Recreation

Safely back in Stranraer after their Canadian adventure, Hammy vividly recalled his first impression of their new acquisition, the North West Castle, the place where he once scrumped apples:

"The whole place was in pretty rough shape. In one room there was a stove in the middle of the floor with a metal pipe going into the chimney. The building had been neglected for some time, and I could see that if something wasn't done pretty quickly, then the whole place might be completely lost. We could see that turning it into a hotel would require some big internal changes."

To create the rooms that would be large enough for a restaurant, as well as have somewhere for a dance floor, walls would have to be moved and floors strengthened. Hammy's extensive building and construction experience gained in Canada came to the fore. He was Clerk of Works, and pitched in alongside the skilled men he'd hired to do the job. He'd known most of them from earlier days, and he was sure that they would turn in some first-class work.

The Deputy County Clerk at the time, D. R. Wilson, recalled going to the North West Castle with his boss in early 1962 to see how the young McMillan boys were getting on with their new purchase. After trailing through the near derelict building, they found them in the cellar of the house exhausted and looking somewhat dejected, sitting on lemonade crates and having coffee out of tin mugs. Hammy asked "Do you think we've done the right thing, opening a hotel?"

"He constantly carries a tape measure with him – I think it ties in with all the work that taking over historic buildings has brought about, and working with tradesmen." (McMillan member of staff)

One week before the doors are due to open...

> **KINEMA CAFE.**
>
> **WAITRESS,** not too young and with some experience; until October approx; also woman for evenings, some cooking, dishwashing.
>
> **WANTED** for new hotel, experienced cook, references required. — Apply Manager, North West Castle.

Eventually they managed to create twelve guest rooms. Two more would become a flat and their home for the foreseeable future. There was much frenzied activity during the winter of 1961-62 as the hotel's kitchen, dining room, bar and reception areas were fitted out, lounges and bedrooms decorated and furnished.

The target was for an April opening, just in time for the long Easter weekend. Despite the distraction of Janet being admitted to hospital for a gall bladder removal, soon after the arrival of baby daughter Fiona, the McMillan family welcomed their first guests on schedule.

There was certainly a buzz of interest in the Stranraer business community about the new venture. Hammy had seen how Canadian newspapers regularly carried advertising features for businesses, something that was quite unknown here. Eventually the *Galloway Advertiser and Wigtownshire Free Press*, Stranraer's

NORTH WEST CASTLE HOTEL

Official Opening By Mr John Brewis

AID TO TOURIST INDUSTRY

IN PRESENCE of a large number of friends, North West Castle Hotel was officially opened yesterday afternoon by Mr John Brewis, MP. Mr Brewis was welcomed by Mr H. McMillan, jnr, on behalf of the proprietors, and after the opening ceremony he presented him with a gift from the family. The company were shown round the spacious hotel which will prove a considerable asset to the tourist industry. There are twelve bedrooms for visit...
loun...
loun...

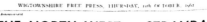

weekly local paper, was persuaded to carry a similar package, timed to appear soon after the Official Opening of North West Castle Hotel on October 3rd 1962. Mr John Brewis, the MP for Galloway, congratulating the couple on their achievement, said that he was sure the hotel's contribution to the local economy and to the tourism industry in the area would be far-reaching. Hammy remembers how the business was now really starting to gather momentum:

"We started to do functions and these were very popular – we advertised our first Dinner Dance in September 1962 and that quickly sold out. Word spread and we got lots more functions that I believe would never otherwise have happened – I remember the Chief of Police telling me that applications for late licences to do weddings and functions went up by a hundred percent every year during the first five years of business. And we didn't have a big ballroom then."

THE NORTH WEST — STRANRAER
A story of initiative and enterprise

THE MANAGEMENT OF THE NORTH WEST CASTLE
invite you to attend a

Special Opening Dinner Dance
ON SATURDAY 13th OCTOBER 1962
(AND EVERY SATURDAY THEREAFTER)

Dinner at 8.30 p.m.   12/6d per person

Please book your table early – Telephone Stranraer 465

For Janet, the wedding trade was to become her major forte. North West Castle quickly became a new focal point for celebration. Brides-to-be, along with anxious mothers, were to discover in Janet a comforting soul-mate who could take away all the worries of planning the reception: the guests, the master of ceremonies, the table arrangements and the banquet; the drinks on arrival and during the meal; the flowers and decorations; the piper and the entertainments:

"I well remember the first wedding reception we had – our experience was very limited then, so we got Willie Bow, the Manager at Western House in Ayr, and who had organised our own wedding reception back in 1960 to come down and show us the ropes! For this first booking we had menu cards and accessories that had the name of a well-known whisky brand printed on them. The only problem was that the guests did not partake of alcohol. So at the last minute all the cards had to be changed and the bottles behind the bar had to be discreetly concealed from view."

Janet still enjoys arranging the wedding receptions along with the North West Castle team:

"Every occasion is a little bit different of course – more so these days – couples usually like to be innovative about their very special day. It's really nice to be able to help them achieve their wishes, and in the good times when it's sometimes seen as fashionable to go overseas for a wedding we have to try and show that we can be just as exciting."

Janet's calming nature and years of experience that she has offered to many hundreds of happy couples is now legendary in Stranraer. Fifty years later she takes great delight at browsing through her archive of original notes made for each of these occasions.

North West Castle bedrooms - 1963 style.

NORTH WEST CASTLE
STRANRAER

Wine List

CHAMPAGNE		Bott.	½-Bott.
1. Heidsieck	...	39/6	22/-
2. Moet & Chandon	...	35/6	18/6
3. Bollinger & Co.	...	31/6	—
BORDEAUX: Red			
4. St. Julien	...	14/-	7/6
5. Medoc	...	11/-	—
CLARET			
6. Bordeaux Rouge	...	9/-	—
7. St. Emilion	...	12/6	6/6
BORDEAUX: White			
8. Barsac	...	14/-	—
9. Sauternes: La Flora Blanche	...	18/6	10/-
10. Marquis De La Rose	...	15/-	—
11. Gilbeys Spanish	...	8/-	4/6
12. El Morano Spanish	...	7/6	4/-
13. Graves: Lauries Blanc	...	18/-	9/6
14. El Morano	...	7/6	4/-
BURGUNDY: Red			
15. Beaujolais 1957 and 1959	...	13/6	7/-
16. Nuits St. Georges 1957	...	19/-	10/-
17. El Morano	...	7/6	4/-
BURGUNDY: White			

HOCK		Bott.	½-Bott.
19. Leibfraumilch Crown of Crowns	...	23/-	—
20. Leibfraumilch Blue Nun	...	23/-	11/6
21. Leibfraumilch Hanns Christof Wein	...	21/-	—
22. Niersteiner 1959	...	15/-	—
ITALIAN WINES			
23. Chianti Vecchio	...	22/-	—
24. Chianti Melini	...	22/-	—
RHONE WINES			
25. Cha'teauneuf Du Pape 1959	...	16/6	—
SPARKLING WINES			
26. Asti Spumante	...	22/-	—
27. Red Burgundy	...	21/-	—
SHERRIES			Per Glass
Walnut Brown			3/-
Bristol Cream			3/-
Tio Pepe			3/-
Dry Sac			3/-
PORT			
Sandeman/Grahams			2/6

LIQUEURS

Advocaat, Apricot Brandy, Benedictine, Cointreau, Cherry Brandy, Creme De Menthe, Drambuie, Glayva, Grand Mariner, Kahl'ua, Kummel, Pernod 45, Tia Maria ... 3/-
Bisquit Dubouche, Chartreuse ... 4/6

Menu

Luncheon   June 1st 1964

Fruit Juice Various
Grapefruit Maraschino
Cream of Green Pea Soup
French Onion Soup

Fried Fillet of Sole & Lemon

Braised Beef Steak
Grilled Lamb Cutlets
Roast Leg of Lamb & Mint Sauce
Cold Boiled Gammon & Salad.
Cold Oxtongue & Salad.

Roast & Creamed Potatoes
French Beans   Brussels Sprouts

Baked Rice Pudding & Stewed Rhubarb
Fruit Salad A La Mode
Peaches & Fresh Cream
Biscuits & Cheese

Coffee

NORTH WEST CASTLE HOTEL
Stranraer

ROTARY INTERNATIONAL
in Great Britain and Ireland
District 102

The Rotary Club of Stranraer
10th Anniversary Dinner

North West Castle Hotel, Stranraer

Friday, 18th October, 1963

Chairman:
Rotarian ALEXANDER HANNAY
President of the Rotary Club of Stranraer

Inaugural Meeting   — 20th August, 1953.
Charter Granted   — 20th August, 1953.
Charter Presented   — 30th October, 1953.

North West Castle - Dining in style in the mid-1960's

With their first year's trading accomplished, Hammy and Janet could see that the North West Castle Hotel had the potential to grow. They needed more bedrooms, and much more space for functions and receptions. It wasn't long before plans for a new extension were being prepared.

Hammy wasn't too keen on the first outline designs:

"They were far too modern in appearance; at that time it was the fashionable style for architects all round the country to submit. I wanted something that would match the character of North West Castle. The planning authority was not too sure about the new building methods either – they wanted to know who was going to build it. I remember my brother standing up in the council chamber and telling them that I'd constructed buildings in Canada that made this new wing look as small as a hen house! He convinced them that I had sufficient experience to do it – and I had."

"I didn't want to see big picture windows and steel frames on the outside."

At that time it was one of the biggest projects of its kind in Stranraer. Reinforced concrete floors on each of the four levels, with single span beams would provide the greatest degree of flexibility in the arrangement of space for the restaurant, kitchen, ballroom and 20 more bedrooms. There was central heating, room telephones, and the hotel car would be on call to meet arrivals from train and boat.

The first extension to the North West Castle was completed soon after the opening of the new ballroom in 1964.

September 1964 brought another red letter day and another grand opening – even though construction was still under way on the upper floors to complete the project. The new ballroom on the ground floor was ready, and the Provost of Stranraer cut the ribbon with great ceremony. Many guests recall how Hammy had to change quickly from brown overalls into a kilt, and swap his tools for serving cloths and spoons!

THE GALLOWAY GAZETTE, SATURDAY, DECEMBER 4, 1965

New Castle Bar Completes Stranraer Hotel Extension

THE ultimate in comfort, cuisine and service is offered by the North West Castle Hotel in Stranraer, one of the finest establishments of its kind in the South-west of Scotland.

The hotel, which is owned by Messrs H. C. McMillan & Sons, was officially opened in July, 1962, by Mr John Brewis, M.P. for Galloway. At that time it consisted of twelve bedrooms, a residents' lounge, public lounge and dining room. Management of the hotel was placed in the capable hands of Mr H. C. McMillan, junr., and his wife.

An enterprising and ingenious young man, Mr McMillan anticipated the ever-increasing demand for accommodation, service and food of the highest standards and with this thought uppermost in his mind he set about the task of renovating.

dance and by popular request, the Smorgsborg will be continued over the festive season.

part of the banqueting suite lies adjacent to the ballroom and is now available to people attend.

IT is mysterious and Bohemian yet quiet and romantic, the sort of place you would expect to meet agent 007 himself. Where is it and what is it? Why it is the new Castle Cocktail bar, one of the most unique in Scotland, the latest addition to the new North West Castle Hotel in Stranraer.

On entering the new bar which opens to the public today, one is immediately caught up in its olde worlde atmosphere, for it is almost entirely constructed of stone. The construction and design of the new bar is unique in as much as most of the stone used is part of the original building.

The stone flooring in the new Cocktail bar has been cleverly laid out in crazy paving fashion and is partially covered with Indian rugs. In keeping with the Dickensian atmosphere of the new bar, the roof is supported by a large stone pillar and slate-like stone beams add to the cavernous mood of the room.

The bar itself must surely be one of the most unconventional

In 1969 the decision was taken to install a lift. Perhaps Hammy's decision to do this had stemmed from his much commented-on trademark greeting of guests – personally taking their bags up to their rooms.

One day, an American guest, on arriving at North West Castle, told Hammy that back home he would be called a bell hop. When Hammy told him that he was called anything from the porter to the proprietor, the guest almost fell back down the stairs. Whether Hammy's varied designations were known to a very special guest in 1969 is not recorded – but nevertheless it was quite an event:

"We got word that Prince Philip wanted to stay here. He was on a shooting holiday. Quite unusual, we thought he might have stayed at a country lodge. We were sworn to secrecy. Part of the Resident's Lounge became a private dining room for his party. I remember they got back from their first day's shooting at about six o'clock. There were quite a few other events going on that evening as well, so there were quite a lot of people about. At first the Royal party thought that there might be a horde of people waiting to see them – so they all decided to go in via the back door. They went in by the kitchen – saying hello to the chef and staff – which they thought was great.

Now if anyone was upset by the fact that they didn't know about the special visitors it was our youngsters. They were all at school, but somehow they'd got to hear about the visitor. So one evening we got them smartly dressed, with the boys in their kilts, and we sat them on a couch at the foot of the stairs. On his way through, Prince Philip spotted them, and went to have a chat – and it fairly made their day!"

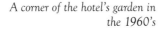

A corner of the hotel's garden in the 1960's

It was the ferries to Northern Ireland that kept the North West Castle Hotel very busy. The *Caledonian Princess* left at seven in the morning, so the breakfast service had to be earlier than in other hotels to enable departing guests to get checked in for the sailing. The same ferry returned at 9pm, bringing another flurry of travellers looking for somewhere to stay. When their hotel had filled up, Janet would telephone all the local bed and breakfast establishments, and so help another important sector of the local tourist industry.

But for Hammy there were ominous signs on the horizon:

"Our trade was buoyant until the start of the troubles in Northern Ireland. The tourist traffic more or less disappeared. More ferries had now come on to the route with sailings throughout the day - so the need to find somewhere to stay overnight also fell away. Mind you, there was an unexpected bonus from the troubles. It was triggered by a newspaper revealing that one of its journalists had made a ferry crossing unchecked by the existing security arrangements. The Stranraer Police Chief came to see me – and told me that the Home Office wanted to station thirty five high security officers at Stranraer, and they needed accommodation – immediately. They came – and they stayed for two years."

One of the hotel's regular guests was a Mr Loudon. Interested in the many developments that were happening at the hotel, he had noticed that there was a plot of land behind the police station, and encouraged Hammy to investigate its purchase. Its eventual acquisition from the police, who owned the ground, was to be another turning point for the enterprise. Britain's road traffic laws were to aid and abet the strategy:

"Barbara Castle, the Transport Minister, had recently introduced the breathalyser. Social drinking, especially as part of other events such as sport fixtures, had been severely impacted. In those days Wigtownshire curlers would go to matches held in the nearest ice rink at Ayr. On their way home they would stop for something to eat and drink in Girvan, and maybe a few other places on the way. But the breathalyser changed all that. Now, when they got to Stranraer, players would have to phone their wives to come and pick them up. There could be as many as thirty, even fifty, such requests. We were delighted to cater for them here of course!"

Stranraer curlers planned to start building their own ice rink on the edge of town. They spoke at length with Hammy about the idea. Then there was news that curlers at the other end of the county, in Newton Stewart, were also planning to build a rink. Considerable controversy erupted between the two sides. When it became apparent that there wasn't any funding available for the Newton Stewart project, Hammy seized the chance and prepared plans for an ice rink at the North West Castle. It was a move that received the support of all parties, and that recently purchased little parcel of land at the back of the hotel would now be very useful indeed.

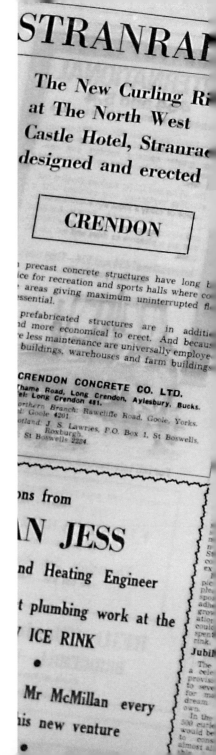

STRANRA[E]

The New Curling Ri[nk]
at The North West
Castle Hotel, Stranra[er]
designed and erected

CRENDON

[...] precast concrete structures have long b[...] [...]ce for recreation and sports halls where co[...] [...] areas giving maximum uninterrupted fl[...] [...]essential.

[...] prefabricated structures are in additi[...] [...]d more economical to erect. And becaus[...] [...]e less maintenance are universally employe[...] [...] buildings, warehouses and farm buildings[...]

CRENDON CONCRETE CO. LTD.
[T]hame Road, Long Crendon, Aylesbury, Bucks.
[T]el: Long Crendon 481.
[N]orthern Branch: Rawcliffe Road, Goole, Yorks.
[Te]l Goole 4201.
[Sc]otland: J. S. Lawries, P.O. Box 1, St Boswells.
Roxburgh.
St Boswells 2284.

[...]ns from

[...]AN JESS

[...]nd Heating Engineer

[...]t plumbing work at the

[...]Y ICE RINK

'S MOST ATTRACTIVE SPORT AM

THE PROVISION of the four-pad ice rink within the down to a main rea of North West Castle grounds, Stranraer, Galloway where en provided with another sports interest in a ...

Official opening of the ice rink - November 1970.

Construction of the ice rink under way in August 1970.

will continue now with the second building programme. As planned, this will be a four-storey, T-shaped hotel, which will join up with the building, which will be an underground entrance to will be the existing car park, leaving a reception area for vehicles

Everyone around Hammy knew that his building and construction experience would come to the fore with such a development. The vital statistics must have seemed music to his ears – 65ft concrete portal trusses; a double lined roof and cavity walls; 4ft deep excavations filled with 2000 tons of stones and topped with 200 tons of concrete; two 50 horsepower compressors pumping 500 gallons of brine and four miles of polythene piping to maintain the ice sheet.

By late autumn 1970 the new four-sheet ice rink had been completed, seven months after the idea was first conceived and only five months after planning permission had been granted. The *Wigtownshire Free Press* trumpeted the inauguration of another McMillan achievement: 'SPECTACULAR' ran the headline. One hundred curlers from the south-west of Scotland converged on a *'picturesque Tyrolean appearance...and who had never before seen [such] an exciting and brilliant decoration as the Alpine scene which occupies the whole wall of the rink.'* They had come to congratulate and to compete for a new trophy, the Drummond Rose Bowl, donated by the Drummond family of Glenside, and which would be played for on the last day of October. The newly formed Stranraer Ice Rink Curling Club undertook all the organisation.

Curlers flocked from all over Scotland to enjoy themselves and this unique new attraction. As the first hotel in the world to have its own indoor curling rink, North West Castle had never been busier.

NORTH WEST CASTLE
STRANRAER

4 – Family Life - and The Roaring Game

A long with all the excitement of the developments at the North West Castle Hotel, the McMillan family was expanding. In July 1963, Fiona was joined by Hamilton; little more than a year later, and there was Douglas. July 1966 heralded Fay's arrival, and in August 1967 she was able to greet her younger sister, Gail.

The two-room flat on the top floor that had been the McMillan family bolthole from the hotel business was now seriously stretching at the seams. Fiona remembers how they coped:

"The flat was pretty basic. It had a living room with a pull-down bed for Mum and Dad. The boys' room was on one side and we girls had the room that's now the Accounts Office. Mum's wardrobe was a cupboard under the stairs. Although the flat was a squeeze for us, I remember Saturday nights when there was a Smorgsborg dinner: the Modernaires Dance Band would be playing and their music wafted upstairs into our flat. When I was supposed to be in bed I used to sneak downstairs in my nightie to listen to the music!"

Five growing and energetic youngsters needed space. Fortunately they were able to find this when they moved a short distance away to a house in Stranraer that had been built by Hammy as a home for his aunt and uncle; they had come back to Scotland on his retirement from the Ford Motor Company in Canada in 1970. At first, Fiona was bewildered by the new environment:

"Although we did once say to my father that we'd like to live in a normal house, when we moved out from the hotel I hated it. I missed everything that went on – especially the buzz of the place and meeting all the different people who came to stay."

Growing up in the hotel environment has been an experience that none of them will ever forget. As Douglas McMillan recalls, in the

Family memories captured during brief breaks in a busy daily routine.

sixties the walled garden of North West Castle was a great open-air
adventure park:

"There was a lot of scope around the grounds of the hotel to enjoy an
adventure or two – making forts or tree houses. There were a couple
of big trees in the middle and my cousin David, who had been a Boy
Scout, built a tree house – it was our own private little world. There
were old greenhouses, and an ice house, as well as one or two scary
little holes that were good for the imagination. There was the odd
rodent, but we didn't seem to mind that! We had pets galore – there
was a dog, a hamster, a goldfish and a budgie as well as guinea pigs.

Fiona, our older sister had a horse stabled in the boathouse. I vaguely
remember using a water pistol on Fiona's horse – it didn't like that

Douglas McMillan - forty years
separate these two pictures.

much, so it broke the door down and went galloping into the town. We kept very quiet about that!"

Being the eldest, Fiona was the first in line when it came to thinking about a possible career:

"When I was eleven I began to work in the dining room. I didn't serve but I would write down the food orders on the checks. I worked in the kitchen washing dishes. Any of my friends that came round helped wash the dishes too! I also helped the housekeeper, Margaret Hermstedt; she was also our nanny. Her husband had been a German prisoner-of-war, and he was now a plumber who did work around the hotel for my father. Their daughter Maria was the first receptionist at North West Castle."

Fiona Hardie works on the McMillan archives.

Hammy and Janet's lifestyle revolved continuously around work and the hotel. Fiona, in her role today as the company's archivist, often reflects on a paradoxical situation typical of many family hotels. For half a century her parents, immersed in making sure that their guests always enjoyed themselves, would have very little time for a social life of their own. While the family was close-knit and supportive, many activities had to play second fiddle to the needs of the hotel. When it came to education, Hammy and Janet recognised this and took the decision to offer the next generation the opportunities of a broad-based schooling away from their hotel home.

For Fiona, the idea of leaving home was a bridge too far:

"I wasn't keen on going away to boarding school – and Mum and Dad didn't pursue it. I remember well the time that I went to a careers evening at Stranraer Academy. Dad came with me; I think he hoped that I would start work in the hotel. I told him that I might consider a career in a bank; I wanted a normal job – like my friends. So he found some leaflets on a stand about Hotel Management and gave them to me."

Fiona left school at sixteen and went to Bournemouth to go on a six-week course to be a hotel receptionist:

"I stayed in digs, it was quite enjoyable; there was a great sense of freedom. I think I might have had quite different views about sending my own daughter away at that age! I returned to North West Castle, and started in reception. It was shift work, and from the very start of my working life I knew nothing else. I moved on into the Accounts office for a couple of years until I got married. Although that brought my career in the hotel business to an end, it's strange how even today you still miss it, especially when you enter through the front door and go up to the reception desk."

Fiona Hardie, on the stairs where she listened to the Saturday dance band.

Maria Hermstedt at the reception desk in 1965.

Hamilton in 1972, and today in the historic Ross Bar at North West Castle

For the other youngsters little jobs and duties continued to be Hammy's gentle drip-feed on the opportunities that lay in the hotel and the hospitality industry. Hamilton and Douglas were next in line:

"Dad used to try and keep us occupied and wherever possible involved with the business. The first paid job Douglas and I did was every Saturday and Sunday morning. We had to clear out all the empty bottles from the six bars that were running – there weren't any mineral dispensers in those days – and we usually had six to eight big skips of empty bottles to sort out. That would take about three hours or so doing that. We were about eleven years old then and we got paid ten pence per hour. Sixty pence a weekend! The worst part of that job was getting to the bottom of the skip where all these bottles had been lying – invariably there was a broken bottle of tomato juice at the bottom. That was our introduction to working life."

At 12, Hamilton was the first to go to boarding school. Merchiston Castle in Edinburgh, with its considerable sporting achievements and location in the capital appealed to him, but the lure of holidays and working at North West Castle remained strong:

"My favourite place was working in the kitchen; it was chef's work for me – doing breakfasts. Sometimes there were over a hundred people staying, and I enjoyed helping the breakfast chef. When I left school I went straight into the kitchen to work. I would have loved to have been a farmer. Mum's background was on a farm, and my Easter holidays were spent up at Auchtralure and at the hill farm at Craigbunoch. I used to go and do the lambing – and when my uncle was ill I did the whole job. After that came the shearing, and I would go and help with that."

Douglas's school adventures appeared to be designed to test the resolve and patience of any headmaster. Describing his prep school near Moniaive as 'pretty draconian', he recollects how he and four friends decided one Sunday to attempt to escape. In something reminiscent of an old Ealing film comedy, they absconded overland towards a friendly house some 25 miles away in Kirkcudbright. The fine weather deteriorated, the daylight faded and the mist closed in. Chilled and short of the kind of food that keeps young boys ticking, Douglas and his companions descended to a road:

"We hoped to thumb a lift. A few hours later the first vehicle that came along was the school minibus... I think we were quite glad to get into it! We were taken to a police road block that had been set up, and then back to school. Letters were sent to Mum and Dad. Mission definitely not accomplished."

Then it was off to join brother Hamilton at Merchiston. No thoughts of escaping needed there: sporting activities and long-lasting friendships ensured that Douglas enjoyed his time before finally deciding that instead of a career in physical education, the hospitality industry might also be his metier. Again, it was the experience gained during the school holidays when he would return to North West Castle to help out that probably swayed him in that direction. Many time-served staff at the hotel still remember when, during a wedding reception, he was given a job to do. The drinks for the wedding toast, the whisky, the sherry, were always kept poured in readiness. On this particular occasion the bridal party arrived early, no drinks had yet been prepared and Douglas was hastily despatched to get the toast ready. Concern grew as the celebratory glasses still failed to appear, and a desperate search finally revealed Douglas hard at work in the kitchen – making a considerable quantity of toast!

For Douglas, the need to explore the world before settling down to work had to be satisfied. With five years' experience in management at North West Castle and the recently acquired Cally Palace, in

Staff Reunion 2012 - Douglas McMillan remembers past events at North West Castle.

1987 he travelled to France and found work in a hotel. In the style of most backpackers he moved on, dropping in and out of jobs, mostly in hotels and catering in Australia, before returning to the McMillan fold in 1989. This was a time when Hammy and Janet were well on their way with an ambitious programme of expansion, and there was a lot of work to be done.

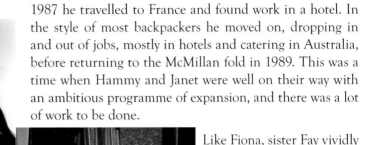

Like Fiona, sister Fay vividly remembers the seven or so years of the cramped flat: "I remember being put to bed early on Thursday nights because there would be a business meeting in the sitting room. My first job was in housekeeping at the age of eleven – I got 15p an hour, £6 a week, which sounds pretty ridiculous today!

Liking food, but not very keen on cooking, Fay decided to stay out of the kitchen, and worked in other departments of the hotel during weekends and school holidays. A degree course in Hotel Management at the University of Strathclyde followed:

"I never imagined that I would do anything else – at school when they asked me about a choice of career my mind was already set on Hotel Management."

After a secretarial course and training in the wine business, Fay was ready to join the family business full time.

Fay in 1972 and today:
"Hotel life was a good introduction for me start at
the bottom, and from there the only way was up."

Youngest of the second generation is Gail. At the age of four, the part-constructed shell of the ice rink and new bedroom block had become an unofficial playground for her:

"My eldest sister Fiona had left home to do a training course. I remember being asked if I wanted to go away to school, and because I was having a great time at home, that didn't really appeal. In the end I did go to boarding school, to St Denis in Edinburgh. My other sister Fay was there, but she was in a more senior house, three hundred yards away, and we could only see one another for an hour on Sundays. So the first years weren't particularly wonderful. But I got used to it."

After school and a final year spent on a secretarial course, Gail came back home to start work at North West Castle.

Gail, above in 1972 and today:
"I had space around me, I had Mum and Dad to myself, and I quite enjoyed that."

left: the Second Generation 'on parade' in May 1985 - Fiona, Fay, Gail, Douglas and Hamilton.

scotch whisky.

STRANRAER ICE RINK
North West Castle Hotel
Luxury 3-star Hotel with own Ice Rink, offering a wonderful new centre for curlers
Open Curling Competitions every weekend, the winners of which will go forward to an end-of-season Competition—
First Prize : A Mediterranean Cruise for four
Special Terms for Weekend Curling Parties
1 Night from £5-5-0
2 Nights from £8-8-0
Ice included
The famous Smorgsborg Buffet Dance or Dinner also included
Phone : Stranraer 2644
Resident Manager : H. C. McMillan, Jun.

With most of the youngsters away for their schooling, Hammy and Janet had a little more time to relax briefly from the business. In the winter months it was invariably the new ice rink that commanded their attention. Hammy was a relative newcomer to the sport:

"I didn't play a great deal in the early days. But I soon picked up the skills – and five years after we'd opened the ice rink, we'd won the Dalrymple Cup, a mixed team competition created by Janet, who was a very keen curler."

The ice rink made up for the business that had been lost because of the downturn in the numbers of visitors travelling to and from Northern Ireland. There was a steady flow of bookings during weekdays, but the weekends were proving more of a challenge.

So Hammy devised a new concept – a weekend curling package, with players staying in the hotel. They advertised on buses, even local ITV. When topped with a big match prize, such as a fortnight's holiday in the Mediterranean, bookings began to flood in. It was almost too successful – after three years and with not all of the rooms yet complete in the new wing above the ice rink, Hammy and Janet found that they were sold out to the point that accommodation with other guest houses had to be booked to cope with the demand.

The family's passion for curling continues unabated to this day. For Hamilton it's still a major passion:

"Curling has played a big part in our lives. Father encouraged all of us to be involved with the sport; Fiona was at one time Scottish Junior Champion, and also won the Scottish Mixed; Douglas and I won the Scottish Open Schools' in the late seventies, and we played in the Junior Finals when we were 15-16 years old. Gail has made curling a big part of her life too – she's made a big success of it."

For Hamilton, curling became really serious in 1981: "That was the year of my first Scottish title – the Scottish Mixed Championship. I was about eighteen then – and three years later I won the Scottish Junior Championships. Then it was into the Scottish Mens'. Stranraer curling has been very successful, with some very well-established teams – and after playing in teams elsewhere for a while I came back and joined them.

We won five European Championships; got a bronze and two silver medals in the World Championships. In 1999 we were in in St John, New Brunswick, for the World Mens' Championship, where Mum was seen on television screens around the world knitting furiously

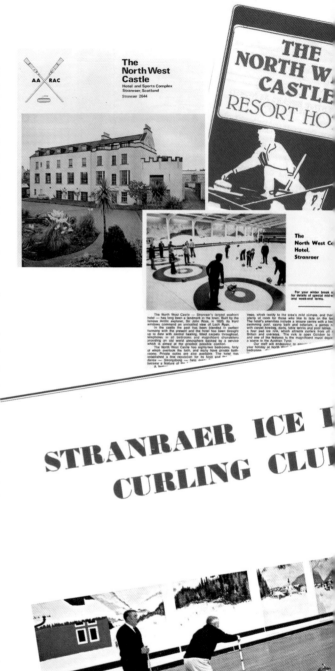

while we battled for the gold, beating the favourites, the Canadians. The host nation weren't best pleased with that result; in fact they refused to wear their silver medals. My father is more analytical – he's a bit more of the old school than Mum– and he often questioned some of my game tactics."

Hamilton considers he's fortunate to have achieved the goals he set himself while still young. After winning the European and World Championships, and having the medals as a permanent reminder of that success, there remained the Olympics – but curling was only a demonstration sport until 1998. He likes to think he could still do it.

Meanwhile, Gail increasingly devoted her now competitive attentions to the Roaring Game, and she has taken over the responsibility of running the ice rink. Organising all the bookings, the fixtures and dealing with curling clubs from all over the country demands a military-style accuracy and attention to the tiniest detail. Over the years, and through the activities of the Stranraer Ice Rink Curling Club, the ice rink has become increasingly attractive to younger players. With curling now an official Olympic event, there has been a significant rise in enquiries for coaching at the rink.

Working alongside a team of coaches, Gail has seen the numbers of local youngsters aged from 11 to 17 years grow to around 250. They help fill the rink for nearly six months and together with all the club fixtures it's statistics like these that help keep the place a hive of activity during the winter. Both Gail and Hamilton see this as a crucial investment in the future of the sport as well as the hotel, sustaining a flow of new curlers to Stranraer well into the next decade and beyond.

Besides fulfilling many roles with the Royal Caledonian Curling Club, Gail has achieved considerable success in the sport, winning with her brother Hamilton the Scottish Mixed Championship in 1988. Ten years later she won the Silver Medal with Rhona Martin in the European Championships, and became Scottish Champion in 2008. That success was capped in 2010 when, again with Hamilton, she won the Scottish Pairs Championship.

One of the first issues of the Royal
Caledonian Curling Club's Annuals,
published in 1849.

5 – Traditional and Friendly

'*T*he *great advantage of a hotel is that it's a great refuge from home life.*' So wrote the Irish critic and playwright George Bernard Shaw.

If there's one characteristic that guests quickly sense on arriving at the North West Castle Hotel it's the feeling of home, of a family atmosphere. Invariably there is a member of the McMillan family somewhere close at hand. The McMillan 'feel' has been nurtured carefully, and the seventies and eighties would see the growth of the business from the original twelve bedrooms to the present seventy-two, as well as the successful addition of the ice rink. All of it undertaken without compromising the local charm which has become a hallmark of the hotel. Traditional and friendly – as Douglas McDavid found during his first job in reception:

"It was 1982 – the most memorable thing was this computer. I'd never seen a computer before. I'm pretty certain that we were the first hotel in Scotland to have one. Mr McMillan was very open to the idea of embracing new technology. When the first fax machines came out, costing over a thousand pounds in those days, he saw the value that they could offer to the business, and immediately bought one. He was the first person that I knew that had a car phone – he could see the potential."

Douglas McDavid's rapid progress with the McMillan enterprise whetted his appetite to gain more experience from around the world:

"I bought a single ticket to Australia. I handed in my notice; Mr McMillan wished me well. I travelled for two years – working in hotels in Australia, fruit picking on farms and meeting an Irish girl who was also travelling and working –and we came back together to Creetown. I'd no sooner got back than the 'phone rang – it

Douglas McDavid

was Mr McMillan, who'd heard I was back. He wanted to see me immediately. I started back at North West Castle, where Hammy's son Douglas was General Manager and, a bit like me, wanted to take time out and see the world. I encouraged him to try it out and off he went to satisfy his wanderlust."

For twelve years, Douglas McDavid captained North West Castle. Working with Hammy they would spend time discussing marketing strategies. With curling packages successfully established, the idea of providing a golf package – staying at the hotel and getting free golf at Stranraer, Dunskey and Cally Palace – was born. Thanks to the Gulf Stream and a very mild climate, the ever-popular and strikingly colourful gardens at Logan, Glenwhan and Castle Kennedy provided the basis for launching a package that would appeal to gardeners:

above:

North West Castle in the 1980's with the new wing at the rear providing a greatly expanded number of bedrooms, housing the ice rink and leisure pool.

right:

following a major refurbishment, a new facade was added in 1992.

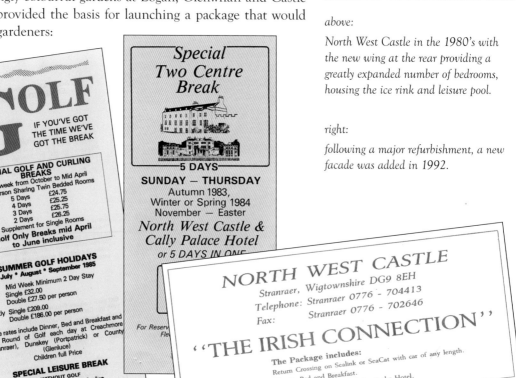

GOLF
IF YOU'VE GOT THE TIME WE'VE GOT THE BREAK

SPECIAL GOLF AND CURLING BREAKS
Mid week from October to Mid April
Per Person Sharing Twin Bedded Rooms
5 Days   £24.75
4 Days   £25.25
3 Days   £25.75
2 Days   £26.25
Supplement for Single Rooms
'Golf Only Breaks mid April
to June inclusive

SUMMER GOLF HOLIDAYS
July • August • September 1985
Mid Week Minimum 2 Day Stay
Daily   Single £32.00
Double £27.50 per person
Weekly   Single £209.00
Double £186.00 per person
These rates include Dinner, Bed and Breakfast and One Round of Golf each day at Creachmore (Stranraer), Dunskey (Portpatrick) or County (Glenluce)
Children full Price

SPECIAL LEISURE BREAK
WITHOUT GOLF
November - June inclusive
2 - 5 Day Mid Week

Special Two Centre Break

5 DAYS
SUNDAY — THURSDAY
Autumn 1983,
Winter or Spring 1984
November — Easter
North West Castle &
Cally Palace Hotel
or 5 DAYS IN ONE

For Reserv

NORTH WEST CASTLE
Stranraer, Wigtownshire DG9 8EH
Telephone: Stranraer 0776 - 704413
Fax: Stranraer 0776 - 702646

''THE IRISH CONNECTION''

The Package includes:
Return Crossing on Sealink or SeaCat with car of any length.
Dinner, Bed and Breakfast.
Use of all the Leisure Facilities in the Hotel.

Hamilton McMillan

"Hammy really did have a vision. He would move ahead on new ideas quickly. When the internet was in its very early days I asked the growing McMillan family what they thought of it. I'd read about it and had seen an example of a hotel in Aberdeen already using it. Within days, we'd found out who'd built the website, and we were building our own. That's why he's so stimulating to work with. Occasionally things might not work out – but he'd never hold it against you, he would simply say 'Let's move on!'"

Today it's Hamilton who's at the helm of North West Castle. Like father, like son? Let him tell his own story:

"I suppose I'm a bit like my father in that I want to get things done – I'll go out and do them and maybe ask questions later. I'm not a great one for procrastination. I hate paperwork. The big difference

with us, compared to a big chain of hotels, is that you will always see us somewhere. I don't bury myself in the office; I'm out front, certainly at just about every function that comes here and in the evening. If I'm needed to be hands-on – I'll serve, I'll do the wine. I like to keep in touch with the guests, making sure everything is as it should be. The hotel trade really does demand a liking for being with people and looking after them."

left:
The North West Castle team today.

right:
Staff Reunion, July 2012.

The biggest asset to any hotel are its members of staff. Many of them have worked here since the very early days, and they all remember with considerable affection the supportive nature of the hotel's owners. Much of the recruitment for the growing hotel was done on a word-of-mouth basis. When the hotel first opened its doors it was a quite simple affair for Janet to look after:

"Mrs Jefferson was our first cook. Apart from the occasional early breakfast request which I looked after from the small kitchen in our flat, she attended to all the dining requirements. The staff that came to work for us in the early days usually stayed with us a long time. Many guests still remember the late Sheila Kirkland, who was with us for almost fifty years. It's been much the same ever since – which is interesting in an industry like ours that has to cope with a high turnover of staff. There are always people, many of them local, who are asking us to be put on a waiting list for a position. In some cases it's a family tradition – we're now on our third or even fourth generation of family employees: grandparents, fathers, mothers, sons, daughters, brothers, sisters, uncles, aunts, nieces, nephews, cousins – all working here."

Twenty-five years after starting work at North West Castle on a Youth Training Scheme, Bruce Maclean quickly rose through the ranks to become Head Chef at the age of 21:

"I started as a waiter – and learned how to do a cheeseboard. The head chef at the time saw that I'd got a bit of a flair for art and

Bruce Maclean, Head Chef at North West Castle and his signature dish - pan fried breast of Gressingham duck, with fondant potato, baby vegetables, orange, honey and thyme jus.

Passing on twenty-five years of experience - Bruce Maclean demonstrates his skills to a new recruit to the kitchen.

design, and he asked me if I'd like to work in the kitchen. Within a couple of weeks of starting here, Mr McMillan knew all about me and about my family. They do like to know everything that's going on – if they don't, they quickly make sure they find out! People talk about staff being loyal to their employers. Here it's also a case of employers being loyal to their staff. They're very fair – if you've a problem you go to them, they'll try and help you."

One of the legacies of the 1970's was a body of highly skilled chefs who had worked with British Transport Hotels. Creative and highly disciplined in their craft, a number of them joined the McMillans and passed on their skills to aspiring staff that would in turn rise up through the ranks. Bruce was lucky in that he came under the wing of Richard Naylor, one of the BTH brigade:

"Richard was very traditional and used to big functions. Later I also went to Kirroughtree House on my days off to learn from their first chef, Ian Bennett. He'd trained with the Roux brothers, so my passion for food largely came from Ian, while the discipline for the job came from Richard Naylor. As a result, I pride myself in that I have one of the calmest kitchens going. There's never a panic."

Most mornings at six-thirty, Ann Paterson, already smartly dressed for breakfast service, arrives at the hotel. After a quick update with the chef she looks forward to greeting the guests and making sure that they have a cheerful start to their day:

"My mum used to work here as a barmaid and waitress. I started as a part-timer with functions, but now that my family have grown up I'm full time. We've had football teams, rugby teams, darts teams, and pop groups staying here; and I remember Geoff Capes, the strong man. There was the film and production crew who were filming the TV serial '2000 *Acres of Sky*'; and then we were full of soldiers for Operation 'Purple Warrior'. Some of our guests have been coming for many years – and they often remark just how like a family it feels when they're here. Some get quite concerned when they don't see you."

Each morning Ann ensures that one timeless accompaniment will be ready for dinner in the evening: "I just love to make the Melba Toast! You'd be surprised how many people are amazed to find that we still have it!"

left & right:
Teamwork at North West Castle.

6 – Growing the Business - Cally Palace

Cally Palace

left:
A calm spring evening.

below:
Wigtown Bay
Overlooking the River Fleet National Scenic Area with the Solway Firth and the Isle of Man just visible on the horizon; the Machars peninsula in the near distance.

The A75 road that heads east from Stranraer and the North West Castle Hotel frequently skirts the shores of the Solway estuary. The shoreline is studded with grassy knolls with clumps of sea pinks and white campion. Unconcerned by the passing traffic, sheep graze on the salt marshlands of Wigtown Bay, while in winter huge flocks of geese that have flown down from the Arctic give spectacular dawn flying displays as they head out to graze the still green pastures. East of Creetown there are tantalising glimpses of bays with miniature archipelagos and distant vistas of the Isle of Man. The huge rolling slope that is Cairnsmore overlooks all of this and the beautiful valley of the Water of Fleet below its eastern flank.

Back in the mid-seventeenth century there was little to speak of at Gatehouse. As the name implies, there was just a single house where tolls on this strategic route to the far west and to Ireland would be charged to defray the costs of a newly built bridge across the River Fleet. In the early 1700's the influential Murray family, owners of the Cally Estate, began the development of the town – a settlement of houses grew up around cotton factories and a brass foundry; tanneries and a brewery; brickworks and a shipyard. Gatehouse of Fleet prospered, and in 1763 James Murray began building Cally House.

Gardens were added and in 1835 an imposing new portico, consisting of four granite monoliths was added. A superb setting for a superb mansion.

Descendants of the Murray family continued to live at Cally until 1933 when the estate and house were sold by Mrs Elizabeth Murray-Usher to the Forestry Commission. With no interest in the building, the state-owned agency sold the house for £2,000 to a hotelier and his wife from Fort William, in the Highlands. The opening celebrations in March 1934 were evidently quite some affair – the hotel was fully booked on its first night; a grand luncheon of mock turtle and asparagus soups; salmon with mousseline sauce and cucumber salad; roast chicken and York ham, followed by sherry trifle heralded a style of hospitality that would set new standards in the area.

The Cally Palace Hotel would have presented a welcome sight to a 1930's traveller from London in search of the wildernesses of Galloway. Inspired perhaps by the adventures of John Buchan, and Alfred Hitchcock's recently released thriller 'The Thirty Nine

Steps', and keen to partake of some shooting or fishing, he (or she) would have alighted at an oil lamp lit railway platform in the middle of nowhere to be greeted by a uniformed chauffeur and brightly polished automobile. 'Boots Meets All Trains' would have been the ideal strapline on any advertisement for the newly opened hotel, some six miles distant from the rather deceptively named Gatehouse station.

For just five years the hotel prospered in this quiet backwater but with the outbreak of the Second World War it became a home of a different kind, and with somewhat noisier residents. Cally House became Britain's first local authority administered co-educational boarding school. Senior schoolchildren and teaching staff from Glasgow were evacuated there to complete their education in as normal a fashion as conditions allowed. A short film made in 1942 for Scottish cinemas, and now in the National Library of Scotland, shows a typical day where youngsters rise bright-eyed to the sound of a morning bell. A strident commentary describes how they organise themselves for breakfast, attend lessons, sports and social events, as well as undertaking the daily chores of housekeeping and tending the productive vegetable gardens.

After the war and the departure of the school, the hotel was reopened. There followed a succession of owners, mainly large corporate conglomerates that had no Scottish connections. By the early 1980's various building and modification works to extend and create more, smaller bedrooms that would appeal to the coach tour business had been carried out.

Meanwhile, back in Stranraer, and almost twenty years since its establishment, Hammy & Janet McMillan's enterprise at North West Castle was doing well. It was time for the family to look at a new strategy. Hammy recalls how his two brothers in Stranraer, both with their successful businesses, were to play a key role in his next big move:

above:
School life at Cally House during the Second World War.

"We knew about the Cally Hotel being up for sale – we'd been to it a few times and liked the look of it. I went to see our local bankers about a purchase, but this was too big for them, and they referred us to their Head Office in Glasgow.

My brothers were able to be the financial guarantors that the bank required. After the usual horse trading, I got the loan that was needed to do the deal with Trust House Forte and buy Cally Palace."

Hammy wanted most of all to see local hotels brought back into local ownership and he was prepared to spend £600,000 to get the Cally. But acquisitions like this usually demanded a degree of discretion, verging in some cases on total secrecy. Hammy's lips were sealed:

HIRE AYRSHIRE CRANES
Telephone: AYR 81931
BARRHILL 279
GLENLUCE 329

GALLOWAY'S TOP SELLING NEWSPAPER

The Galloway Gazette

AND STRANRAER NEWS

NEWTON STEWART, Saturday, 26th September, 1981

Per Annum. Ireland £15.60, Abroad £18

Vol.112 No. 6,022

Registered at the Post Office as a Newspaper

Gazette exclusive

Hammy takes over the Palace

ONE OF South-West Scotland's biggest and most exclusive hotels changed hands in a major investment deal signed this week.

The 90-bedroom Cally Hotel in Gatehouse has been bought by Mr Hamilton McMillan, owner of Stranraer's North West Castle Hotel.

Mr McMillan clinched his impressive purchase on Monday . . . . and announced immediately the old 'Cally Palace' name would be restored.

"I'm delighted to have acquired such a fine country house hotel," a happy Mr McMillan told us.

Sellers Trust Houses Forte have had the 18th century building and 100 acres of ground on the market "for some months" according to a spokesman.

"We are very pleased with the outcome, and glad the staff are all to be retained," commented Mr Rodger Burney, area director if T.H.F.

Mr McMillan and his wife Janet met the Cally's thirty members of staff on Thursday, and hinted more jobs could be

ly not — one is enough for anybody."

Mr McMillan made it plain the Cally Palace of the future would be very much for the people of the area, as well as visitors. Dinner dances every weekend of the year are to a feature as the new boss seeks to establish firmly the

Hammy and Janet McMillan at the Cally Palace Hotel yesterday.

"At that time our children knew nothing about this. We decided to have a quick break as a family and on the way back to Stranraer we stayed a night at the Cally. A few weeks later, we told them that we'd been shopping. They asked what for. I kept them guessing. It took them a while to guess that it was a hotel. Then they asked which one. We told them it was the Cally Palace. Their response was unanimous and pretty blunt: 'Not that dump!' I had to admit the accommodation was not particularly good. But I knew that we could, and would do much, much better."

One key member of staff who was recruited in the early days of the Cally Palace's new ownership by the McMillan family was a personable young man from nearby Creetown. Recently qualified in hotel management, Douglas McDavid was all set to go abroad on a skiing holiday in Europe when he picked up a copy of his local newspaper. The headline 'Hammy takes over the Palace' stopped him in his tracks:

"There was a picture of Hammy and Janet sitting outside the hotel; at first I couldn't believe a family from Stranraer had bought the place from Trust House Forte. What's more, I soon learned that THF had taken virtually the whole management team with them. In the meantime the McMillans had put in a 20-year old graduate, Shona Rankin, who'd been at college in Glasgow at the same time as me, to run the Cally. So I called in to see her, and within four days I was working there, doing breakfasts, lunches, dinners. They were short of a chef in the kitchen so I pitched in there as well."

Douglas didn't realise then that this move would be where his career in the hospitality industry really took off. As described earlier in this book, Hammy McMillan spotted the potential and moved him to North West Castle where he would rise to General Manager.

above:
Painstaking restoration work was undertaken throughout the Cally Palace.

In 1981, Cally Palace had all the signs of an occupation by a corporate owner who had ceased to care about the place. Unloved and unwanted by the grey mandarins in London, two wings of the hotel had been closed down. One of these, a modern extension known as the Chapel wing, had seventeen small, single rooms. Now unusable, consent was obtained to demolish it. Painstaking remodelling of the other wing to provide comfortable suites went on for a further two years. Restoration work continued throughout the hotel, in particular the Bow Lounge. Staff remember that it was something like Michelangelo, with a man lying on his back, on a tower, painting gold leaf onto the ceiling cornices and decorations.

Cally Palace

The Bow Room with its magificent gilt cupola ceiling.

Hammy was keen to imprint the McMillan style as quickly as possible. Cally Palace was going to be a quite different place – a jewel in the south west of Scotland. A new, enclosed swimming pool replaced the outdoor facility. He was also concerned about the low standard living quarters that were available for staff:

"We completely renovated these, providing ensuite rooms, all with their own front door. To get and be able to hang on to good staff these days you have to provide them with good accommodation."

The view to the south-west and the Cally Lake.

Cally Palace is situated within the River Fleet National Scenic Area and the award-winning Cally Designed Landscape. The grounds immediately surrounding the hotel had been in the ownership of the Forestry Commission, and Hammy realised that there was great potential here:

"The Forestry Commission had a nursery in four parcels of land, and they decided to sell these. I knew that if I could acquire these there would be enough space to build a golf course. A neighbouring farmer also agreed to sell me a few acres needed to complete the 18 holes. I gave him a membership, and he's still a member today. I knew that having a golf course here would be a major attraction – it would be comparable to the ice rink that we'd opened at North West Castle. It would be a private course that would bring in guests, who could have a relaxing time with none of the pressures of a club."

The bid to buy the land was lodged with the agents at the last minute. Hammy and Janet delivered the paperwork personally to Dumfries, just to make sure. In the early nineties they started construction. A leading golf course designer from Ireland, Tom Macaulay, who had a considerable number of projects to his credit, including a course at Gleneagles, was appointed. The works were to take two years; by 1993 the works had been completed and the course was then rested for a year so that it would be ready to open the next season.

Peter Madeley, who is now the greenkeeper for the Cally Palace golf course had been looking after the gardens and grounds for eighteen months before the hotel was taken over by the McMillan family:

"When Hammy decided to build the course and asked me to be the green keeper, I jumped at the chance. But a short time ago I had to have a heart transplant; Mr McMillan and his wife were always asking for me and how I was recovering during the eight months that I was away. They reassured me

that my job would be there for me whenever I was able to return – and it was. You can talk to him – he's always there if you need him. If something isn't right you can be sure it's not long before he's there!"

All year round the fairways and the greens are expertly manicured by Peter and his team:

"Golfers want a smooth green, and one that's got speed. Our greens are well drained, but we can irrigate if things do get very dry. Recently we calculated that around 10,000 people walk across the greens during the year, so the soil gets compacted; we need to fertilise and water it and generally give it the tender loving care it needs. If it doesn't get that it tends to bite us back! During the winter we do any alterations, cutting back scrub, attending to areas that need the drainage improved, and patching up pathways and roads. When spring comes the greens are rolled and top-dressed; the cutting programme gets under way so that everything is nice and tidy for the golfers. Towards the autumn it's a matter of tidying up and putting everything back to bed for the winter. There are no handicap rules. It's a super course, very quiet – there may only be 30 or 40 people a day here; you can see red squirrels or roe deer; you have time to relax, play a few or all of the holes in your own time or just have a knockabout."

One of the greatest challenges to face Hammy and Janet in the days immediately after they took over the Cally Palace was the recruitment of staff to manage the hotel. It has to be said that the McMillan 'nose' for people with the right skills at the right time is second to none. It was possibly something of a surprise in hotel circles when they appointed a young woman from a Whithorn farming family first to be an Assistant, then a full Manager at the tender age of 21. Jennifer Adams trained in Hotel Management at Duncan of Jordanstone College in Dundee, and after a spell in Inverness came to Cally Palace. She began working with Hammy and Janet on the extensive programme of refurbishment works in addition to running the hotel. Right from the start she appreciated the vital role of the team behind the scenes. Wherever possible Jennifer would recruit from within, enabling many of those who started as youngsters to work their way up – from washing glasses or dishes to head waitress, or head chef. It was her belief that this approach fostered strong loyalties, a deep sense of mutual respect and a sense of fairness amongst the staff - all of which resonates with Hammy and Janet's outlook.

'The Boss', as Hammy is known throughout the business, is renowned for his hands-on approach to the business. Marjory Harper has been a housekeeper for over thirty-five years:

"There was some building work going on. He had a beautiful suit on, he took his jacket off, he had the braces for his trousers, brilliant white shirt, and I look down and he's got the wellies on. 'Right then boys, that's the ready-mix done, let's get stuck in!' On another occasion we were getting a carpet delivered for the new wing and the van bringing it broke down. We'd only got the underlay down and all our guests were starting to arrive. Hammy was there with his braces on, getting all the suitcases together and taking them up the stairs. He always had to have hands on. He had vision – he'd talk quietly to you: 'We're going to knock down

above:
Monitoring water quality in the
Cally Palace leisure pool.

opposite left, and right:
Ready for action!

the fifties! We're going to knock down the seventies!' But always there was a concern for you, and your family – if one of them is unwell, he wants to know about it."

Through the years the hotel's managers have observed the impact that familiar faces in the staff have on returning guests. It's become a tradition of the hotel that guests and staff follow each others' progress – perhaps a new child or grandchild one year, an exam success or a graduation achieved a decade or so later.

One couple who have achieved what is almost certainly the record for numbers of visits to Cally Palace are Stuart and Dorothy Fairclough, from Bolton in Lancashire. For over twenty years now they have come to stay at the hotel every month – and in 2001, in recognition of their loyalty, Room 71 was renamed *The Fairclough Suite*. Stuart, a retired dairy farmer, whose mother came from the south west of Scotland, discovered Cally Palace quite by chance. The pair were so enamoured by the place that they decided they wouldn't go anywhere else. The ever stronger friendships between the Faircloughs and the hotel staff have led to some extraordinary gestures. Janet Taylor, who works in the hotel's restaurant, recalls a very special occasion as she planned her wedding day with her fiancé David, who is Cally Palace's smiling, multi-tasking porter, housekeeping assistant, dishwasher, and who can also be very handy on the maintenance side as well:

"Mr and Mrs Fairclough got to know about our wedding plans, and one day they asked me if they could come to my home to take me and my father to the church with their car. It was a lovely surprise, especially when they brought a second car for my sister and my nieces. It was a frosty winter morning, with the sun shining brilliantly, the cars had been washed and polished at the back of the hotel and made ready beautifully. The Head Chef baked us a wedding cake and the hotel's flower arranger did the icing."

DAILY EXPRESS MONDAY MAY 21 2001

NEWS

Suite dreams for hotel's regulars

BY IAIN LUNDY

A COUPLE who have spent more than £30,000 staying in one hotel, have had their favourite room named after them.

Stuart and Dorothy Fairclough arrived for their most recent break at the Cally Palace Hotel in Gatehouse-of-Fleet, Kirkcudbrightshire, to discover room 71 – where they always stay – was renamed Fairclough Suite.

The couple, from Bolton, Lancashire, have been coming to the hotel every month for the past 10 years.

It is estimated they have driven 17,000 miles and stayed for more than 100 nights and spent around £30,000.

They are as regular as clockwork. They are our best and most loyal customers by far," said manager Douglas McDavid, who presented the couple with a plaque engraved with "The Fairclough Suite" to hang outside their room.

The retired couple, who farmed near Bolton, once tried another hotel in

Scotland but got "homesick" and checked out after two nights. Mr Fairclough, 67, said: "We had not had a holiday for 30 years and I thought my wife deserved one and we were driving through Gatehouse-of-Fleet and saw this place. Now we come every month.

"We had such a wonderful time that we decided we would never go anywhere else – and we never have."

The Faircloughs now spend four days every month at the 56-bedroom hotel, from Thursday to Sunday and take a 10-day summer holiday there every year.

Mr Fairclough said: "My mother came from the South west of Scotland, and I really feel it is my spiritual home. The people are so friendly and we have made a whole different life for ourselves up there.

"We nearly bought a house up here, but, decided we would miss staying in the hotel too much."

HONOURED GUESTS: Stuart and Dorothy Fairclough flank Cally Palace Hotel manager Douglas McDavid

above:

Douglas McDavid presents Stuart and Dorothy Fairclough with the commemorative plaque.

below:

Stuart Fairclough shares wedding day memories with David & Janet Taylor.

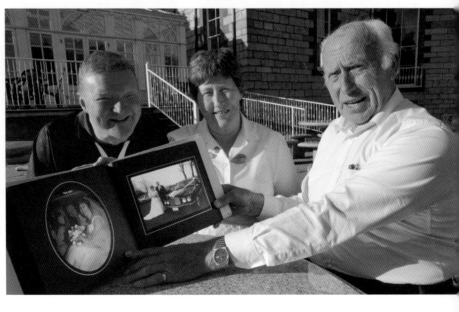

Cally Palace, with its magnificent surroundings, had considerable potential for weddings. Hammy McMillan decided that when Jennifer Adams left to get married, Douglas McDavid should move there to start building the wedding business:

"When I came to Cally Palace from Stranraer I introduced the concept of the wedding package. We had some beautiful accommodation and our reputation for fine dining had put the hotel on the map, especially during the summer months. During the winter we were much quieter, and that appeared to offer the best opportunity to provide exclusive use of the hotel for special occasions such as weddings. Big house parties like that kept the wheels turning when otherwise we would have had to close."

As business increased Douglas McDavid's team was also augmented. Bob McWhir had worked in many of the McMillan hotels, but was now enjoying life on the high seas with the Cunard Line. While cruising off Norway's Arctic coasts and islands, a telephone call from Douglas was to persuade him to leave the world of the Captain's Table and fine dining on board the *QE2* to re-join the team. Bob, a local man from Gatehouse of Fleet, and Cally Palace's General Manager enjoys extending the welcome that's been Hammy McMillan's philosophy from the very first day:

"I eat, drink, sleep, think hospitality all the time. To be successful I think you have to give your life and soul to the job. It's a bit like a theatre: the audience – our guests – are there to be entertained. I'm responsible for making sure that the show goes on and that they get a good show. Guests soon notice if the manager's not about; there's something missing as far as they're concerned. That's something that Mr McMillan is always on the ball with – if he hears that there's been a problem with a room, or service, he'll make a personal visit in very quick time to sort things out. He's very hands on."

Bob McWhir,
General Manager, Cally Palace.

Bob McWhir's career started in hospitality when he was fourteen – washing dishes or working in the restaurant in the evenings and at weekends at Cally Palace. At eighteen he decided to go full-time and went on an in-house training course for Food Service under the wing of Douglas McDavid. He regards that as the best hands-on experience he could ever have had, preparing him for his next globe-trotting experience, working with Cunard.   He regards Cally Palace as the ideal situation for a youngster embarking on their first job:

"They're living on their own, but they're still in a secure environment, which is very reassuring for parents. I recruit young staff in very much the same way as I began. You start at the bottom – dishes and pots, then move on to veg preps, and so on. It's not just youngsters – there are several older employees here who are on work placement, doing NVQ's. That usually happens when families have grown up and they've got more time and energy to devote to gaining qualifications."

below:

Head Chef Jamie Muirhead harvests wild garlic from the Cally Palace grounds.

Below stairs, Head Chef Jamie Muirhead is busy with a young team, bringing on their skills and aptitudes; in his spare time, and with the blessing of the McMillans, he's an Assessor for Dumfries and Galloway College:

"I really enjoy being able to teach, to pass on my knowledge to those who are keen to make their way up in the industry. At the moment I'm training up a young lad to become a sous-chef. He's worked with me for a while in the kitchen and he's ready to start the next big stage of his training. I reckon he'll be there by next year. You can usually see very quickly if the potential, the capability to take on the next level of responsibility, is there."

As a youngster living in Thornhill, Jamie was always interested in cookery, but his school careers advisor tried to persuade him that he might be better at metal or woodwork. He stuck to his ladle however. After a spell at college in Dumfries he was able to gain

below:
Training for perfection in the kitchen.

Seared Kirroughtree venison, with celeriac, wild garlic, fondant potato and rosemary jus.

some excellent kitchen experience in the Lake District. It wasn't long before his talents were spotted, and he started as second chef at the Cally:

"The menus have evolved over the years – increasingly the emphasis is on seasonality of produce. When each new season begins we do a careful review of what worked on previous occasions. I enjoy meeting Mr McMillan and discussing the menus. Recently I did a dish based on lamb which I'd brought from the Lake District. Mr. McMillan wasn't too keen on it however. He told me to take it off. Some months later it reappeared, and when he came in for dinner one evening he questioned its return. The General Manager at that time, Douglas McDavid, told him that the Dining Room had been raving about it. He left the room with a smile on his face and he's never mentioned it since!"

The Team Spirit at Cally Palace

Loch Trool - *Galloway Forest Park*

7 – Kirroughtree Adventure

Between Gatehouse of Fleet and Stranraer lies Britain's largest area of forest. The Galloway Forest Park was established in 1947, and encompasses not only valuable commercial forests but huge tracts of wild, open moorland and some of south Scotland's highest hills. 'The Highlands of the Lowlands' is an apt soubriquet.

There's plenty of unpopulated space here – something of great appeal to the visitors who come each year. Some will be coming for the immensely popular mountain biking trails – The 7stanes. Others are homing in on Newton Stewart – a centre for walking that brings scores of rucksacked and booted groups from all over the country and further afield to enjoy the uncluttered slopes, landscapes, coastlines and forests of Galloway, now a UNESCO biosphere, the third of its kind in the British Isles.

The lack of urbanisation has resulted in the genesis of a new tourist pursuit – stargazing. Britain has very few areas where the skies are unpolluted by mile upon mile of street lights, illuminations, signs and floodlights. That wonder of the heavens, the Milky Way, is usually concealed in a fume-laden amber haze. In the Galloway Forest Park, the land of Dark Skies (virtually unique in Europe), all is revealed. Touting telescopes and warmly wrapped against a chill night air, visitors come to marvel at the sights that hang above their heads: galaxies, stars, planets, satellites and the occasional shooting star; maybe even a wintery glimpse of an aurora – the northern lights. Indeed, what they see will be little changed from the skies that would have enthralled our national bard, Robert Burns.

Burns was a regular visitor to the area and to Kirroughtree House in particular. The Heron family had lived here since the house was built in 1719. Their ancestors, who went back to the time of William the Conqueror, were wealthy cattle traders. The mansion was a visible statement of their success. When Patrick Heron was seeking election as the Whig candidate for the Stewartry area, Burns wrote three Election ballads in support of a successful campaign. Recitals of songs and poetry around the imposing staircase, perhaps even a little dalliance upstairs would have accompanied the patronage – in all a useful supplement to his official duties as an exciseman. In his footsteps, and a generation of the Heron family later, followed the young diarist and poet James Boswell, who: '*rode 12 miles upon a hard stoney road, encompassed with high mountains, mostly barren and rocky. We got to Kirrochtree about 3 o'clock, and had a very kind reception from Mr & Mrs Heron and Lady Kames.*' Poetry aside, in all probability it was the newly-married Mrs Heron who was the willing subject of Boswell's attentions, with the oak panels bearing silent witness.

In the late nineteenth century the house and lands were subsequently sold to become a sporting estate and Victorian wings and turrets were added to the building. Eventually, in 1952 the owners sold Kirroughtree and it became a conventional hotel with bar on the outskirts of the market town of Newton Stewart. There were a succession of owners, and a loyal staff looked after the 27 rooms.

Up to the early nineties Yorkshire owners Mr and Mrs Henry Velt had been turning Kirroughtree into an exclusive country house. Its location, strategically placed between North West Castle at Stranraer and Cally Palace at Gatehouse was perfect as far as Hammy McMillan was concerned:

"You could call me a bit of an opportunist – when Kirroughtree House came on the market my interest was aroused. I looked at the place, and I knew that a lot of work would be needed there."

Kirroughtree House and the portrait of its most famous visitor, Robert Burns.

The all-important grades that are awarded in the hospitality industry, and that are increasingly demanding to attain, have always been at the vanguard of the McMillans' objectives. In the early nineties, the next generation of the family had become major players in the development of the enterprise.

Douglas McMillan, who'd spent time travelling around the world and working in hotels had returned to Scotland, and with his wife Susy saw the potential that Kirroughtree offered:

"Although we had 4 Stars at North West Castle and Cally Palace, we knew that a three red Star rating was much better. With Kirroughtree we knew that the location was exactly the type of place that could reflect a higher grading. Award-winning service combined with award-winning cuisine. When we bought the hotel it was in reasonable condition but it wasn't red Star standard – so we undertook a phased programme of gutting floors, remodelling, putting rooms back to original shapes and sizes, creating more spacious accommodation."

From the twenty-seven rooms, seventeen emerged. The work was to take about five years, with most of the work done during the winter months of January and February when the hotel closed for the winter break. All these efforts brought recognition in the form of three AA red Stars, two AA Rosettes and RAC Blue Ribbon Awards. Hammy remembers the first year of work, when the dining room was restored:

"We took all the bench seats out, and had one big bonfire, but the fire was so big we had to call in the fire brigade – we were concerned that it would set light to the trees behind!"

left:

Echoes of a time when the pound in our pocket seemed to go a lot further!

Kirroughtree House is one of those places that ooze an atmosphere of stylish yet informal hospitality from the moment you begin the drive up the azalea and rhododendron-lined approach.

Jim Stirling, who joined the McMillans at their newly-acquired Cally Palace, and after learning 'from the bottom up' at big name hotels in Torquay and the north of Scotland, took over the running of Kirroughtree House in 1992:

"At the age of fifteen I didn't have a clue what I wanted to do – but then I told my parents that I quite fancied the hospitality industry. They encouraged me to go away and work in a hotel for a short period to see if that was I really wanted to do. Within a fortnight spent working at Stonefield Castle at Tarbet I knew that it was the right decision."

Jim is insistent about the need to keep a solid core of locally recruited staff. Guests, many of whom return here year after year appreciate the continuity of seeing familiar faces. It adds to the feeling of family. In an industry that is renowned for an almost continual churn in staff, the McMillans have become something of an exception:

Jim Sitrling,
General Manager, Kirroughtree House

"We're very fortunate in that in my nineteen years here at Kirroughtree I'm only on to my third Head Chef. That's practically unheard of in this industry. I like to keep the same staff. They know what I want and they get on with it. And because I'm not always changing staff I don't have to recruit and train all the time."

The location of Kirroughtree House, tucked away from the main road to Stranraer and with a commanding view out over the Machars peninsula and Wigtown Bay, was perhaps an unintentional bit of strategic planning on the part of the McMillan family. It's an extremely useful location when the weather turns nasty in the North Channel, the unpredictable stretch of water that divides Scotland and the island of Ireland. Before she came to Kirroughtree House as Assistant General Manager, Kate McClymont spent several years working on the ferries:

"I hated April – that was the worst month for high winds. I see quite a lot of guests here at Kirroughtree House who first got to know the McMillans at North West Castle on their way to or from Ireland. A few of them come here for the first time because the ferry sailings have been disrupted by bad weather. Now many of them return for a longer holiday."

They also like to come to golf, walk, fish, shoot, or just rest and recharge the batteries. Kate has seen the numbers of people coming to the area increase too, attracted by biking and star gazing:

"One of the joys of this place is the return business. You know who's coming, and as soon as they arrive, it's almost as though it was yesterday that they were last here. Some people have been coming here for thirty years, even before the McMillans took over the hotel. Many have been regulars at our other hotels – and quite often they happen to meet up with Mr McMillan on one of his visits. A lot of our guests say to us 'It's like coming home', we're really pleased to see each other again."

Matt McWhir, Head Chef:

"I want my food to look good without being overfussy in style – and it has to taste good; freshness is all-important."

The stairway and entrance hall at Kirroughtree House proudly displays a wall crammed with year-on-year hospitality achievements. It's confirmation of the creative teamwork that exists, much of it out of the sight of guests. Head Chef Matt McWhir came a couple of years ago after passing through the kitchen ranks of the Cally Palace under the wing of Jamie Muirhead. He's aware of the big challenges that face him as only the third leader of a talented and versatile team:

"I'd never thought of being a chef when I was young, and it was only while I was working in the kitchens at the Cally, and seeing the dishes going out that I started to get interested. It excited me. That was at age 16 and I've been lucky to make so much progress so quickly. I'd come from commis chef up to junior sous chef. It's a big challenge, but I enjoy it.

We're very lucky in that we have some excellent suppliers close by - local venison, pigeon, game, salmon, fish and seafood all feature on the menu at Kirroughtree, and it's marvellous to be able to work with such fine produce."

A tempting start to a meal -

Ballotine of Scottish salmon, wrapped in herbs, served with shallot and chive cream cheese.

It's the ability to be versatile and adaptable that counts in places like Kirroughtree. When Maxine Ferguson began washing dishes at 14, like so many others who have started at the bottom in the creative atmosphere of a busy kitchen, she soon began to understand how food could be so exciting:

"I used to see them plating up the dishes and I used to taste everything – even if it didn't look as though I might like it. When one of the chefs moved on I asked Mr Stirling if I could take his place – he said that I didn't have any qualifications but that he would train me, and he gave me a chance in the kitchen. It's the best thing that's probably ever happened. Some people don't consider a career in the hospitality industry to be worthwhile. I think that here you can learn so much – it makes you a much better all-round person. Tonight I've got the opportunity to do the sweets: poached pears with homemade ice cream and butterscotch sauce; a fruit sablé with Chantilly crème; and a white chocolate parfait. The hours are different but I can still make time for my friends on my days off. I want to focus on my work – and make something out of life."

Acquiring the skills of the hospitality business - from pots and dishes to housekeeping; to the heat of the kitchen and the calm of the dining room.

The Team Spirit of Kirroughtree House

Portpatrick

above:

An Edwardian postcard of Portpatrick.

opposite:

Portpatrick waterfont, with the Fernhill Hotel on the hillside above.

8 - Portpatrick Ahoy!

In 1826, a young couple wait anxiously on the windswept harbour of Donaghadee on the coast of County Down in Northern Ireland. They're planning to elope to Portpatrick, some 21 miles away and in all likelihood endure a stomach-churning experience on the daily packet boat. They know that once across they'll be able to take advantage of Scotland's rather more liberal attitude to matrimony. For in Portpatrick, known as Ireland's Gretna Green, they could find a Church of Scotland minister who, for £10, would undertake a quick ceremony, seemingly without too much regard for the publication of banns or period of residence. Sadly, they were some 150 years too early to bring their celebration to the Fernhill Hotel, where they could have enjoyed their ceremony and all the trimmings in much greater comfort. A welcoming drink, superb food and a spectacular view across to the Ulster coastline over the bowl-shaped harbour would have added the final touches.

Portpatrick had for many years enjoyed the status of being the main Scottish port for Ireland. But the west-facing harbour and shipping were vulnerable to storms and costly damage, so in 1849 the decision was taken to move the mail and passenger services to the port at Stranraer, which was already handling goods and livestock.

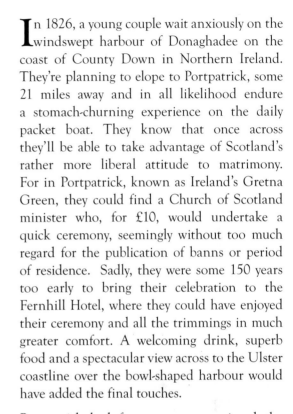

Portpatrick

left:

the village and harbour as seen from the Fernhill Hotel.

That did not stop the construction of a railway line connecting the village to Stranraer and the main lines to London and Glasgow, the first service commencing in 1862. The works for this were enormous and still visible today on the flank of the southern cliff at Portpatrick is an enormous gash, where a final cutting brought the single line around in a huge arc from the north. The harbour became a popular excursion destination where engines would chuff energetically to haul trains of considerable length up the gradient to leave the station.

The house that eventually became the Fernhill Hotel, with its magnificent view of Portpatrick harbour and village, was built in 1872 by a factor of the nearby Dunskey Estate as a private home.

Later it was converted into a private hotel by Mr & Mrs William Purves – a large vegetable garden and glasshouses providing much produce for the kitchen. Guests would have had to travel to Portpatrick by motor car or bus after the railway line was closed in 1950. Around the same time as the McMillans started in business at North West Castle in 1962, the hotel was taken over by Anne Rintoul, later Mrs Hugh Harvie. Over the years Hammy and Janet were able to watch that enterprise develop, and when the Harvies retired in 1988, Fernhill was added to the McMillan stable.

Telephones—PROPRIETOR 220. VISITORS 331. Proprietors—Mr and Mrs WM. PURVES.

FERNHILL

Private Hotel
Portpatrick
By STRANRAER

Portpatrick

The harbour light, with the Fernhill Hotel overlooking the picturesque village.

above:
Ailsa Buchanan,
General Manger, Fernhill Hotel.

below:
A place for stylish relaxation.

Thirteen more bedrooms overlooking the harbour were added as part of a major extension and redevelopment programme. The hotel quickly gained popularity, especially with golfers keen to play one of Scotland's most dramatically situated courses. Stretching along the cliffs and inland, the Portpatrick Dunskey Golf Club's eighteen holes have the additional challenge of distraction from the spectacular views to Ireland, the Mull of Kintyre and the Isle of Man.

The visitor season is relatively short at Portpatrick – and a seven-week winter shutdown enables a planned programme of refurbishment to take place. It's a small enough place for most of the staff to live locally, and when there are special events taking place such as a reception or wedding party, then staff from North West Castle can easily support the house team.

Ailsa Buchanan came as a youngster from Arran to the Rhins peninsula when her father, a shepherd, found work on the gently undulating slopes where the sea is never far away. Before coming to Fernhill as General Manager, she worked for thirty years in Stranraer at Jean P. Ralston's china shop, the last ten of these under the ownership of Hammy and Janet's youngest daughter, Gail.

For Ailsa, the great appeal of Portpatrick are the opportunities for walking. Portpatrick is a destination of some renown in that it's the western 'terminus' of the Southern Upland Way – until recently Scotland's longest wilderness footpath:

"I enjoy walking the Southern Upland Way – I can take the bus to Stranraer and walk back. The last bit of the walk along the coast from Killantringan lighthouse is especially spectacular. We see quite a lot of walkers who start here and walk the various stages of the 212 miles to the East coast. Quite a lot come from the opposite direction – by which time they're ready for a bit of relaxation and a celebration at having completed the whole route.

Killantringan lighthouse -
looking north on the Southern Upland Way.

Mull of Galloway lighthouse -
Scotland's most southerly landfall. The Isle of Man is just visible on the horizon.

Equally spectacular are the sheer cliffs that announce the very end of Scotland at the Mull of Galloway lighthouse. The cliffs here are a huge hotel for seabirds – in the breeding season the vertiginous ledges are packed with noisy, seemingly quarrelsome guillemots and razorbills. Jostling for space above them are kittiwakes and fulmars, aerial artistes that swoop and hang on the updraughts. Far below, glossy black cormorants compete for their own bit of space out of harms' way, whether from above or from a crashing wave.

The drive to Alba's Land's End is not to be hurried. There are fascinating diversions to Gulf Stream-warmed secrets, including the world-famous Logan Gardens. Port Logan with its curving bay and circular watchtowered pier offers shelter from the exposed western seaboard. The road zig-zags from west to east and back, with more stunning views to the east across the more tranquil Luce Bay.

Port Logan

The Team Spirit at Fernhill

Besides the bird watchers and the walkers, Ailsa looks forward to welcoming the golfers:

"There are groups of golfers, ladies and gents, who come to get away from their partners; then there are garden breaks – the Logan Botanics, Logan House, Dunskey, Glenwhan, Ardwell, and Castle Kennedy. Some come here to research their family history – visiting old churchyards and looking at headstones in the hope that they might find a missing relative from a long time ago. That's where having local staff really helps – they know the district well, and a lot of the history."

The hotel's small team takes pride in its versatility – exemplified best perhaps by Alan Paterson. On each of his workdays he drives across from Dunragit to be – in no particular order – a porter, a housekeeper, a gardener, a general maintenance man, even a window cleaner and waiter! Like so many other staff in the group, he enjoys getting to meet the guests, and catching up with all the news on their return visits.

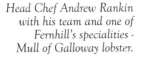

Head Chef Andrew Rankin with his team and one of Fernhill's specialities - Mull of Galloway lobster.

It's a similar situation with the kitchen team: Andrew Rankin, Fernhill's Head Chef left school at 16, and wasn't really sure what to do. He started work in the kitchen at Fernhill under its previous owners; food was part of life at home and his mother also worked at the hotel. He worked his way up through the ranks, including a three year finishing spell at Kirroughtree House as a sous chef. Now he tells everyone that food became a way of life when he came to Fernhill in 2005.

Glenapp Castle, Ballantrae.

9 – Restoration, Restoration

Graham & Fay Cowan

Glenapp Castle

opposite:
A postcard from Glenapp Castle in the late 1930's.

Just south of the Ayrshire coastal community of Ballantrae, the village immortalised by Robert Louis Stevenson in his book '*Master of Ballantrae*', a small and unassuming country road backtracks from the main A77 highway that connects Stranraer and Ayr. There are no signs to reveal what lies in wait for the traveller. Indeed, the mystery continues for several hundred yards until a lodge house and immense Victorian gateway come into view. Glenapp Castle is coy – she does not give up her secret beauty easily. She likes to know about you in advance so that everything is absolutely perfect when you arrive. A discreet call from the phone outside the lodge and, silently, the gate glides open. It's all quite mysterious, and it's very, very different from the prospects that faced Fay & Graham Cowan in the early nineteen nineties.

Fay, the fourth member of Hammy & Janet McMillan's family was all set to travel round the world:

"I met Graham, a vet who was practising in Lockerbie. He decided to make sure that I would come home from my travels by asking me to marry him! After we married, I carried on working at North West Castle, while Graham continued as a vet at the practice in Lockerbie. The two occupations weren't ideal in that the hours were totally incompatible with each other. So we started to look at properties, including a few ruined châteaux in France, where we could start up a hotel business on our own account. Graham wanted to leave his profession and start something new as well. We looked at several places closer to home in Scotland, then in 1993 we found an advert for an unnamed, spectacular Victorian property in South Ayrshire. We showed the picture to my father, to see if he knew anything about it. The following Sunday, he asked us if we'd like to go out for lunch."

It seems that lunch went on the back-burner. The McMillan expedition into somewhat uncharted territory motored through the open gateway, weaving its way up the very long and seriously potholed driveway. The surrounding overgrown woods that obscured any tantalising views retreated only as the party rounded a corner to reveal Glenapp Castle. Graham, who has always been passionately interested in old buildings as well as the furniture that belongs in them, sensed that here they were onto something quite special:

"It was a completely breathtaking sight – a forgotten place – a sleeping beauty, like the castle in the fairytale that slept for a hundred years. In its heyday it had been the domain of James Hunter, the Deputy Lord Lieutenant of Ayrshire; then home to the Inchcape family, who had made their fortune in shipping. An American family followed them, and in 1987 the last owner was from Japan. Things then started to go downhill. The lawns had become meadows and the paths merely suggested themselves by a dip in the ground. The windows were black and peeling and many were completely rotted away like missing teeth. The huge oak doors hung loose and creaking on their hinges. That day we stayed only a little while, but we were completely hooked. Nothing else would ever come close to this."

A viewing with the caretaker was arranged. Fay and Graham, overwhelmed by the beautiful oak panelling and the fine cornice-work in the enormous rooms, knew that the restoration of Glenapp would be their challenge; one that they were prepared to commit to:

"It took a long time to resolve a purchase with the lawyers. There were times when Graham and I thought that nothing was going to materialise. Eventually a deal was struck, based on a lease with an arrangement to purchase. Our part of the bargain was to embark on a programme of restoration of the property, and after five years we exercised our option to buy the castle. It was at times quite

surreal – we never saw the owners again; apart from submitting records of all the work and costs that had been involved to their agents, that was it – Glenapp was ours."

Their first year was spent 'camping' in the master bedroom, along with four electric fires, a four-poster bed with its own chandelier, and a geriatric Springer Spaniel. Despite the fact that they were living alone in a deserted castle, Glenapp was home and they were delighted to be there, with the whole process of restoration becoming one of total fascination for Graham:

"A great deal of time was spent getting the myriad of planning consents needed. At one stage we applied for a grant from Historic Scotland, but later we withdrew from that. The processes that would be involved would actually cost us more than the funding that would be forthcoming. There were other impractical conditions such as a requirement to open the Castle to the general public. In the first year here we worked and we struggled with the South Ayrshire planning department. It took just over a year to get thirteen relaxations that were needed as part of the restoration work – such as one staircase being one centimetre narrower than the regulation width for a fire stair. The Secretary of State for Scotland had to approve that. The authorities eventually began to realise that we did have the best interests of the castle in mind, and a lot of the work that was being undertaken was to put the building back into its original state."

In just as poor a condition as the castle were the thirty acres of garden and woodland; it took several days to clear a way into the walled garden; the greenhouses alone needed three months of joiner work and hundreds of panes of glass to restore:

"It was quite different to being a vet. Maybe it was the foolishness of youth but it never entered my head that we wouldn't be able to see this project through. My father-in-law Hammy was the number one source of help and advice right from the outset. His experience and his wealth of contacts were very reassuring. In particular within the hotel group there are a number of specialist and highly experienced people behind the scenes who are responsible for the maintenance and fabric of the properties."

Fay and Graham had to gain knowledge quickly on a myriad of building techniques: repairing stonework, windows and making roofs watertight. Where would the radiators go? What kind of bathroom equipment? What about the existing water supply - was it adequate? What drainage would be required for the property once it had opened as a hotel - a complete new installation would be needed. David Hardie, Fiona's husband, was able to bring a wealth of expertise in undertaking these works, as well as ensuring the structural integrity of key areas of the castle. Road access, the gardens, greenhouses and estate management all presented their problems. There would be a daily barrage of queries and snags to sort out: electricians needed to know where basic facilities such as power sockets would be required - something of a challenge when the room layout and furniture placement still had to be decided.

Every room in the castle had to have the cornices repaired. Luckily there was a talented local craftsman who'd previously worked in the film industry building studio sets. He skilfully repaired the cornices, making new moulds and incorporating the new casts as and when they were needed. And then there was the small matter of a family...

"Our first son, Kerr, was born in 1996 and was often carried around the semi-derelict castle while Mum or Dad did whatever was required that day. We moved back into our apartment on the top floor of the castle at the end

*The immense amount of work required can be
seen from these photographs taken in 1994.*

of 1997, and very soon afterwards, the opportunity was taken to purchase the castle outright from its previous owners. Our second son Ruadhan was born a couple of months before we moved back in. Graham and I worked all day and all evening, seven days a week, 365 days a year. Sometimes we weren't off the premises for weeks on end. We certainly couldn't converse on any other subject, which must have been very boring for our families and friends."

Graham and Fay now had a castle for a home and for their future business. They still had to furnish it.

"During the restoration period Graham and I went to almost every fine furniture auction in Scotland and occasionally to Cumbria. Sometimes we got a pretty frosty reception at these auctions. The regular dealers thought that we were trying to muscle in on their trade, so they would bid the prices higher and higher in the hope that we'd go away! Eventually it became easier and we ended up with several huge rooms at the castle stuffed with furniture and paintings - so much so that nobody could get in to decorate the rooms. We had to spend endless evenings shifting it all from one room to another - sometimes on our own - but occasionally some unsuspecting victim could be coerced into helping."

As the Millennium arrived, and everybody wondered anxiously if their computers would suddenly cease whirring and go into meltdown, Graham and Fay knew that they were at last on the final lap of their restoration project. A countdown of just fifteen weeks remained before Glenapp Castle would open its doors:

right:
The Colquhon Dining Room at the start of restoration work, and today.

"We bought the pieces we loved in the knowledge that if we loved them we would find a home for them."

"Fay and I vividly remember carrying large chests of drawers and wardrobes from one room to another and back again. It doesn't seem to matter that much what the tape measure says about whether or not a piece of furniture or a painting will fit in a space. You have to actually see it *in situ*. It either looks right there or it doesn't, and if it doesn't, you get to carry it somewhere else! We were still hanging up paintings at three in the morning on 20th April 2000 with the first guests due to arrive ten hours later. It was a very surreal moment as we stood in the entrance hall waiting for their cars to appear at the door, all the time our minds racing, trying to figure out if we had forgotten anything. I used to have a recurring dream about having forgotten to buy the silver cruet sets for the dining room. Luckily Fay had that one covered, and there they were!"

There was hardly any advance publicity for the opening. In retrospect, Graham and Fay are pleased that it happened like that, without huge fanfares, so that the very small team – a receptionist, one chef, one housekeeper, one front of house, and themselves could get up to speed gradually, and make sure that they got it right. It's probably just as well they did because three weeks after the opening, Fay noticed that an intriguing guest had signed in:

"He was quite unknown to us, and on departing asked us about our venture. It eventually transpired that he was the General Manager of one of a handful of hotels in Britain that are members of the exclusive Relais & Châteaux Association. He'd come to inspect us; a few days later he wrote saying 'Don't change a thing!' Within a very short time we received an invitation to become members of the Association, and for the rest of the season there were visits from other hoteliers who came to make their own assessments of us. Through Relais & Châteaux we've made some excellent friends and when we go to the annual congresses we can network, meet like minds, get new ideas and advice. That can be especially valuable for advancing our staff as well as ourselves. It's an honour to be part of it."

Today the long driveway up to the Castle is dappled with sun – the woodlands that once encroached and cast gloom everywhere have been tamed. A red squirrel might scurry unconcernedly as Glenapp Castle, with an avenue of bright green hornbeam trees in attendance, finally reveals herself. Befitting of a home that possesses a special welcome, the 'family' – the team that is Glenapp – is waiting at the doorway. John Orr, the Castle Manager, has been with the McMillans for most of his working career:

"It's an interesting mix of guests that we welcome here at Glenapp. The sheer variety that you meet keeps it fresh – you never know who might be next. "It could be an Eastern European oligarch with a retinue of security agents.

Or it may be a couple who've come here from the Central Belt of Scotland or from Galloway for a one-night special celebration for their anniversary.

Either way we want them to feel at ease quickly so that they are not overawed with the surroundings, and can relax. Quite often there's an element of surprise that's been attached to their visit – so it can be quite an emotional time, and it is sometimes for us as well!"

John studied Tourism and Business at Dumfries College. He thought he would end up in a job with the tourist board back home in Northern Ireland. However, after starting at a hotel in the Lake District and journeying home one weekend to Ulster by bus, he noticed the entrance to the Cally Palace at Gatehouse of Fleet. By chance they were advertising at the time and soon he began working under Jennifer Adams as a Junior Assistant. It was there that he met and married one of the staff, Tanya, a receptionist. They planned to move on to new jobs in the Lake District; packed and ready to leave, they said their farewells to Hammy:

"Mr McMillan happened to mention that Glenapp Castle had been purchased, and told me to keep in touch. That was quite a seed to sow in my mind. A few days later a management position became available at Kirroughtree House, which I knew would be much more like Glenapp in character. So we didn't go south, instead we bought a house in Newton Stewart and we worked at Kirroughtree for a couple of years before coming to Glenapp full time in 2003."

John's second-in-command is Hugh McDowall, another McMillan recruit:

"To this day I'm still not sure whether Mr McMillan had a talent-spotting agency but back in 1989 just after I'd finished college I got word that he would like to see me. At North West Castle I met Douglas McDavid and I ended up getting a job there. I also worked at Kirroughtree House, and at other hotels in Ayrshire, but eventually I found myself back at North West Castle as Deputy General Manager. However I really wanted to be in business on my own, so I bought a restaurant in Stranraer. The day after I left the North West Castle Hotel, Mr McMillan phoned: 'How have you spent your first morning self-employed?' I told him that I was away buying filler to fix a window. 'How much was that?' he enquired. 'About £6.99', I replied. 'Where's the money coming from? You haven't even opened your doors. That's you in overdraft already!' That was sound advice – I had started with an overdraft, and here he was already pointing it out to me! He's extremely knowledgeable and helpful, even outwith hotels – if you had a problem at home and explained it to him he'd show you how to fix it."

For Hugh however, the McMillan 'lure' was to prove irresistible:

"I was overjoyed when I got the chance to work here at Glenapp. I've always wanted to work at this level - a country house style, working to perfection, yet in a quite laid-back way as well."

"*We want everything to be absolutely right, but to be relaxed about it as well.*"

More akin to a small ship's galley is the kitchen. Brightly lit and compact, this is where Glenapp's Head Chef and four-man brigade create some of the best dishes ever to grace a Scottish dining table. Discreetly, but proudly displayed around the hotel are the coveted awards confirming excellence – including a Michelin Star and four AA Rosettes, one of only five restaurants in Scotland.

Adam Stokes grew up with food at home: his father wasn't a chef, but he would cook for the family on a Friday night with music turned up loud on the CD and produce fresh from his Peterborough allotment. It was an attitude of mind that was passed on to Adam who, with excellent London-trained tutelage at his college, went on to work his way up, learning and acquiring his skills from some of the best chefs in the country. At Glenapp his dishes exhibit his singular, and highly creative approach:

"The dishes are playful, they're fun. I don't want the dish to be immediately obvious what it is when they sit down. I want them to eat through a dish and discover. There's a signature dish here that's been particularly successful for us – pan-fried foie gras with haggis, potato, neep and saffron purée, and apple. When you look at it, it's not haggis, neeps and tatties at all. A little ball of haggis in a potato ring, hollowed out on the plate. With the foie gras there are caramelised apples, hazelnuts, and an Arran mustard sauce. It's a simple marriage of Scottish and French ideas – a combination of the rich and poor – foie gras and haggis from opposite ends of the culinary spectrum. Neeps and saffron – exactly the same. Though it might not be appreciated as much elsewhere in the country, it's the sort of dish that suits here really well."

And then comes the punch line:

"It's been served to a Michelin inspector and it's helped us to gain four rosettes too."

Adam Stokes:
"I want the guest to be excited by what they're eating. I want them to be enthused."

Terrine of Foie Gras with Smoked Ham Hock, Roasted Hazelnut Dressing and 'Piccalilli' Flavours

The welcoming party at Glenapp Castle

Borders landscape east of Peebles

10 – Borders Adventure

Journeying up from England on the high roads north it's all too easy for visitors to Scotland to rush on over the border and completely miss one of the country's best kept secrets – the Scottish Borders.

Gentle rolling countryside and secluded valleys with intriguingly styled tower houses reveal a land that is distinctly different – there are forests and some superb rivers and lochs to gaze down upon and there is plenty of heather. But you might struggle to find a kilt-wearing kenspeckled worthy in and around the cluster of towns that were once the hub of the Scottish weaving and textile industry. The Borders are quite different from the Scotland that is the clichéd feature of shortbread tins.

It's a landscape that has inspired some of our greatest writers, poets, thinkers, artists and musicians. Even the most unfamiliar eye can quickly detect that the land here is in good heart. Surrounding the mystical twin peaks of the Eildon Hills, guarding the southern flanks of the historic town of Melrose, are patchworks of fields that are testimony to the hard graft of Border farmers. The River Tweed, its origins high in the hills to the west, and close to the border with Dumfries and Galloway, sinews its way past Peebles, Innerleithen, Galashiels, Melrose, St Boswells and Kelso before entering the countryside that since the 15th century has been a subject of 'debate', changing hands between Scotland and England over a dozen times.

Like the great majority of towns in the Borders, Peebles owed much of its prosperity to the woollen industry. Much of that former productivity has now disappeared. Today's population looks mostly to Edinburgh, about forty minutes drive away, for employment. Until the Beeching Axe fell in 1962 on the railway lines that connected Peebles with Edinburgh and the south

to London, two stations served the town. These opened it up to the growing middle class of Victorian population that could afford to get away from industrial grime and pollution. The railway network was vital for the development of a new attraction: situated on a hillside on the northern side of the town, the Peebles Hydropathic Spa had been built. In 1881 its doors were opened to the first of two hundred guests eager to 'take the waters'. The massive sandstone structure, French Renaissance in style, and five floors high, cost over £70,000. (In today's terms, and based on average earnings, that's over £29 million!).

The Victorians were particularly attuned to the expanding scientific knowledge of their times. This new age of discovery encouraged the blossoming of theories, some of them sound, some more questionable, about the benefits of hydropathic treatment. Increasingly fashionable, the Peebles Hydropathic, or Hydro as it had become known, had a team of knowledgeable doctors and assistants, who administered water cures and other treatments – many of these introduced from the flourishing spas and health resorts of Europe. The baths could be based on a variety of materials – among them peat, sulphur, eucalyptus, or brine, and given as vigorous douches in apparatus that resembled the most creative minds of a Hammer horror movie. Water for the curative treatments came from St Ronan's Well, a few miles to the east of the Hydro. Those who had come to partake of the treatments would be recommended to sip a glass or two when they rose in the morning and again a short while before meals.

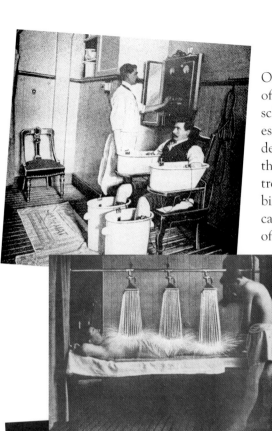

Other medical treatments included the application of poultices of mustard, chilli or hot volcanic mud to help relieve gout and sciatica. The Hydro could generate its own electricity, which was essential for a whole armoury of devices in the electro-therapeutic department. In her fascinating history of the Peebles Hydro, the writer Heather Thom describes many of the appliances and treatments rendered, some of which might be considered rather bizarre in the light of today's medical knowledge. Residents, who came for a week or perhaps even a fortnight could avail themselves of the many facilities on offer – indoors there was a swimming pool ('Swimming Lessons Given') and a huge conservatory. There were more private refuges where gentlemen could pursue billiards or relax with the help of tobacco. Outside there were tennis courts and a cycle track, and the gardeners and groundsmen would be kept busy with greens for bowling and putting.

Some visitors are recorded as being pleasantly surprised at the food on offer, not at all like the Spartan fare that could be encountered at other hydropathic establishments. There was a kitchen garden, and a German chef with a sizeable brigade that would work with all the local produce that could be mustered, within the bounds of seasonality. Duck, partridge, pheasant and other game would often grace the menus, as would a wild salmon or two that had been persuaded, prised and perhaps even poached from the waters of the Tweed just below the hotel.

It was all a highly successful enterprise which went devastatingly wrong on Friday evening, 7th July 1905.

A fire in the kitchen chimney rapidly got out of hand; it was windy, and it wasn't long before the fire alarms were sounded. Guests assembled on the front lawn. They were to have a grandstand view as the horse-drawn Peebles fire engine arrived and then struggle with the impossible task of bringing the outbreak under control. Water supplies were limited, the contents of swimming pool had been used up and hoses were taken up to the Hydro's own water tanks. With the top floor now ablaze, guests were attempting to get back in to the hotel to rescue whatever belongings and valuables they could. Staff began removing paintings from the walls to bring them outside. The hotel turrets collapsed noisily amidst walls of flame and great clouds of smoke.

The passengers of a passing railway train had a spectacular view of the goings-on. Word quickly spread around the town of the conflagration. Hundreds of sightseers flocked to the grounds to watch: 'What a marvellous fire for making toast', a young boy was heard to shout. There were calls to Edinburgh to see if their brigades could assist, hoping that the appliances could be moved rapidly by special train – but that was of no avail when it was discovered that the railway line had already closed for the night and the signalmen had gone off duty. By morning, the Hydro was a smoking, blackened skeleton. The town of Peebles reeled from the shock – the economic repercussions would be serious for so many businesses serving the Hydro.

Phoenix-like, the Hydro was to rise once more, and it all happened with remarkable speed. In just over a month the owners had submitted plans for a new hydropathic. The Glasgow architect James Miller had been commissioned to lead the project with a design that could use the foundations and any remaining elements of the original building that had escaped the inferno. The red Dumfries sandstone which had cost so much for the first construction would be reused – and this was to reflect in a much reduced cost for rebuilding of £37,000 (about £12 million in today's terms). In March 1907, the new Peebles Hydropathic ceremonially opened for business once more.

Peebles Hydropathic Fire—The Ruins, July 1905

Peebles News Series

Calamities such as this were the frequent subject of postcards, often printed and sent within days of the event.

Peebles Hydropathic.

During the First World War, the Hydro was requisitioned by the authorities to be a convalescent home for injured naval officers. Motor transport increased, and the popularity of the Hydro remained high right through the thirties. Hot and cold water became available in all bedrooms in 1926. There were visits by the famous – the singer Caruso, the writer Rudyard Kipling and the playwright George Bernard Shaw among them. It was all very stylish and formal. A place to be seen in.

When the Second World War began in September 1939, once again the Hydro was taken over by the military. Over one hundred and thirty Edinburgh Territorials arrived by train to begin the process of packing up all the hotel's beds, carpets and silver, all to be stored elsewhere so that a substantial hospital for servicemen could be established. Some 1200 beds were installed; in the ballroom, on two floors of the Hydro and also in marquees that had been erected on the front lawn. Peebles Hydro was now a military enclave, with all the attendant security. Similar hospitals had been set up in other large houses of the Borders – Floors Castle, Mellerstain, and Monteviot House.

As the autumn of 1943 flamed its profusion of golds, reds and yellows in the leafy hillsides around the Hydro, Nursing Officer Brenda McBryde, newly recruited into the Queen Alexandra Imperial Military Nursing Service (Reserve), arrived at the 75th British General Hospital – *aka* Peebles Hydro. This was just one of several hospitals that were to be based at the Hydro, where soldiers, doctors and nurses would be trained for operations closer to the front line, wherever that might be. She recalls in her book 'A Nurse's War' how the place echoed to the clatter of Army boots: 'the ballroom bristled with Tobruk plasters and the Balkan Beams of an orthopaedic ward'. The Regimental Sergeant Major appeared to enjoy 'toughening up' what he considered a bunch of over-indulged women. Route marches with gas masks, battledress and tin hats were the order of the day. Lectures on how to treat typical battle injuries were graphic to the point of extremity. Soon after the Hogmanay celebrations that welcomed in 1944 were over, the entire medical and nursing teams all assembled into the ballroom, then known as the Concert Hall, to be told that they were moving on by train to another location. Although they didn't know where, or what they might be going for, this was the long build up for the Normandy invasion.

After the war, the hotel was handed back to the two families that had been its owners from the twenties. It still retained an air of refinement, coupled with the new self-indulgent life-style that characterised the post-war years. Visitors no longer came to seek cures for aches, pains and other ailments, but were more than content to enjoy walking, riding and other activities that might satisfy the senses without acute discomfort. The spa's clinical function ceased.

That did not diminish the very strong atmosphere of 'family' that existed at Peebles for the next half-century. This and the very special qualities of the building and its location were exactly what the next owner would be looking for.

Hammy McMillan remembers clearly how the Peebles Hydro came into view:

The ballroom in its wartime role as a hospital ward.

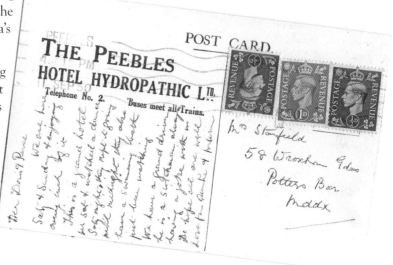

"The hotel had been in private ownership since 1926. Just like us it was also a family business and largely self-financing. In 2004, when increasing health problems began to challenge the directors and with no one in the wings interested in continuing the business, the time had come to look for a potential buyer. It was our accountants William Duncan and Co., who brought it to my notice. They were looking after the Hydro and everyone realised that here was a business opportunity for us and an exit strategy for the owners. It was well-known as a health resort, and there was a good conference and family holiday business. I thought it had potential – a big structure, with concrete floors. I'd read about the first Hydro burning down, so I knew that fire was very much in their minds when it was rebuilt in 1905. That was also my builder's eye on the place!"

It was a big move – and the family didn't know anything about it until the deal had been done. Mindful of how Cally Palace had come into the fold, it really appeared to be a case of Hammy once again working true to form! Hammy wanted the changeover at Peebles to be as smooth as possible. He was confident that the McMillan hotel philosophy would be a perfect fit – with Hammy's son Douglas, later joined by his wife Susy, and Fay and Graham Cowan managing the transition.

Douglas recalls the early days:

"It was certainly challenging – in 2004 we were unknown in that part of Scotland. With 132 bedrooms it's now the largest hotel in the McMillan group. Just down the road and closer to the town is the Park Hotel, a sister hotel to the Hydro and for those who prefer a quieter atmosphere."

Takeovers can be unsettling times for the staff of any established business. When news of the sale was announced at a meeting arranged by the previous owners, and the McMillan family were introduced to everyone, there was the expected ripple of uncertainty. Issy Nairn, Peebles Hydro's Conference Manager recalls how they were soon reassured:

"I suppose there was a level of anxiety. Who were the McMillans? How would things run? In the event, there was nothing to worry about, they were another very nice family and they were very nice to work for. There have been little changes, but nothing major, and the family atmosphere has been kept – there was no overpowering corporate atmosphere – that would have spoiled it."

Caroline Raeburn has worked for many years at the Hydro. Starting as a student, working there in her holidays and gaining more experience around the country before returning to Peebles to work her way up through the Hydro's management team, she is now Deputy General Manager:

"The change of ownership did come as a bit of a shock to us all. We were all called in to a meeting and perhaps the most reassuring thing was that it was another family that was there – it wasn't a big corporate conglomerate that was taking over the Hydro. The majority of our staff stayed on after the change. In many ways not a great deal has changed – we see the Directors each week, they come here and talk

with the staff and together we get the things that need doing done."

The sheer scale of Peebles Hydro can't really be appreciated until a leisurely stroll from one end of the airy hallway to the other is undertaken. It's good indoor exercise when the weather has clamped down outside, and you never know who you might meet on the way! Front of House staff will tell you in a matter of fact manner about the miles, yes – miles, that they clock up over the unique vine and thistle motif carpet in a single day. It can take quite a while, more so if there are stops for the window displays, and a well-deserved pause at the lounge for a mid-way coffee stop.

At the far end of the hall is the grand dining room, superbly proportioned and with a small

"Thirty years ago the hotel was more formal in its style – the Managers wore morning suits in the evening; there was always a strict dress code for dinner" -

(Long-serving member of staff)

Deputy General Manager Caroline Raeburn (front, centre) with the Peebles Hydro Management & Reception Team.

Angus Macleod:

"There's nothing nicer than greeting someone who was last here a year ago – the guests remember that."

stage, grand piano and aspidistras – a superb echo of the twenties and thirties – but just as timeless today. Greeting new arrivals and old friends for dinner is Angus Macleod – the genial, unflappable Assistant Restaurant Manager who has an elephantine memory for names, faces and family history. It really is quite charming to arrive and before long find yourself bringing Angus up to date on your past year's activities and highlights:

"Remembering the names of guests has become something of a speciality. In the dining room you have to find out names. I even did a course that taught me how to do this. I know it works, because even after a day off I'm able to switch in again without any difficulty. The fact that we get a lot of repeat business also helps.

And you remember where returning guests like to sit; maybe a gentleman prefers a nice head to his pint of beer, or someone who has difficulty walking or being seated – all these little things add up to the overall experience."

When the McMillan family took over the Hydro, Angus was working in the bar:

"When I heard that the hotel had been sold I was very pleased to learn that it was another family involved. They spend enough time here to see what's going on, and they give you enough leeway for you to do what's needed. 'Management by Walking About' is vital in making the difference between average and excellent. Douglas McMillan moved me almost immediately to the restaurant to work with Iain Clark where I would then meet 100 per cent of the people coming to the hotel – not just those taking a drink."

As the Hydro's Restaurant Manager, Iain Clark has to exhibit all the versatility of a stage artiste - his days are rarely the same,

below:

Attracting new recruits: Restaurant Manager Iain Clark passes on the skills of table service.

Iain Clark,
Restaurant Manager

Correen Dickson-McCallum,
Restaurant Supervisor at Lazel's bistro.

but the strict disciplines that any team requires to do its job are well laid down. The training and assessment of waiting staff – in silver service, table etiquette and personality when dealing with a guest is critical to the overall and often lasting impression they will take away:

"About 6 pm we get the booking sheet from reception, check that against the table plan; allocate staff to stations, check with the chef that the menu's OK, check for special diets. Half an hour later the staff arrive for a menu briefing and they make sure that their stations, their *mise-en-place* is all OK. On Fridays they get an update on what's happening over the weekend, as well as plans for the week ahead. If it's going to be very busy we forewarn them, especially the part-timers, that they may well be needed. Then we see the dinner service through, and wherever possible prepare for breakfast the following morning."

There's an air of theatre about all this – as Head Waiter and team become stage hands, deftly moving tables, chairs, floral decorations and all the paraphernalia needed for a conference or a celebration:

"Saturdays are invariably quite different – there may be a reception to prepare for. That's when we tend to be a cross between a restaurant and Pickfords! Moving all that gear keeps you fit. There are not very many big waiters in this restaurant – I'm really looking after their health!"

The size, facilities and impressive location of Peebles Hydro puts it high in the league of venues that are suitable

The Bannockburn Room

for conferences and corporate events. This is a very competitive business market – more so in times of economic downturn. Persuading an organisation or large enterprise to forsake the bright lights of a city venue, or move away from holding an event in-house, is a challenging task for Issy Nairn. She started in the hospitality industry in Denmark, and came to the Hydro in 1980. It was quite a different place then:

"At that time we in Reception had our own dining room – we didn't mix with the rest of the staff, we were classed as a little bit more elite! You wouldn't have gone out with anybody from the kitchens! When I arrived there were about 200 staff – there were people in the kitchen that polished the pots, the silver, and the cutlery; there were lots of different jobs around the place."

As Conference Manager, Issy has to ensure that any planned event will run to schedule, often over two or three days. Rooms, technical facilities, receptions and drinks, menus and meal times all have to be agreed with both the client and the supporting departments in the kitchens, bars and elsewhere in the hotel. A conference one week, a large wedding the next:

"Weddings are very special events – the bride-to-be is often already stressed, some of their ideas may just be a little impractical and you have to be really tactful in advising them on alternatives. The first face-to-face meeting is always a great relief to the bride – they know then that there's someone who can make sure things happen, and who they might even need to confide in. Recently we had a two-day Indian wedding which filled the ballroom on the first day with magnificent colours and costumes, and the next day was filled with tartan and kilts in true Scottish style. If that isn't theatrical enough, then every October, on the weekend that we go back to winter time, we have the Scottish National Operatic & Dramatic Association Banquet & Ball. Then the whole hotel becomes an informal theatre and even our staff have an opportunity to discover what stage talents they might have!"

Heather Waters is all too familiar with the ebb and flow of guests that come to the Hydro – she's the Head Housekeeper, and has worked her way up through the ranks over the past twenty-five years. Previously she had endured the humdrum of an office job, and looking for alternative work discovered

Issy Nairn, Conference Manager

Heather Waters, Head Housekeeper

Heather Waters: "It's like the Forth Bridge used to be – you start at the beginning and when you get to the end you start all over again!

the Hydro could bring some buzz into her life. She now manages an inventory of bed sheets, tablecloths and napkins that runs into thousands of items; cleaning materials are bought by the pallet load. Her daily routine means starting at 6 am, scrutinising all the bookings – departures, new arrivals, extended stays – so that she can prepare the work programme and all the linen requirements and supplies for the teams that will start work an hour later:

"Weekends are the busiest times – a lot of people arrive on the Friday night and depart on the Sunday morning – so there's a great deal to be done to get the rooms turned around, completely cleaned and replenished. You're continually forward planning – 'Have I ordered this? Have I done that? Have I got that ready for this Conference? Have I got the right amount of table linen? Have I scheduled enough staff?' I'm also keeping an eye open or anything that needs attention – a door handle or a chair with a problem, batteries for the tv remote control, and I'm always on the lookout for a cobweb! The teams are very helpful and proactive – they will often make suggestions that help our performance. I really enjoy the job – I meet a lot of people. I would meet a family and they'd brought their small kids. Now I see those kids with their children – it's a fantastic family within a family."

Down below in the kitchens, a stock pot continually simmers. This is where the 'taste trail' for every good meal begins. Gordon Murphy, who's been the Head Chef at Peebles Hydro since 2007 started his career on a Youth Training Scheme attachment at Prestonfield House in 1986. In reality, he started at home when he was only ten years old. His CV is impressive – gaining experience through the ranks, and a reputation in the process at Cameron House, as well as in Canada, France, Edinburgh and the Borders.

He enjoys re-interpreting classic dishes – wherever possible taking the ingredients and presenting them in a quite different way. The traditional Scottish cranachan is one such example:

"I've taken the recipe and broken it down into its components – using raspberries, oatmeal, Drambuie in a jelly; it looks much more interesting than the usual whipped creamy cranachan. Sometimes deconstruction techniques work, sometimes they don't, so you have to be careful; you don't want to change it too much or diners won't recognise it."

Ray Jones recently retired as Executive Head Chef with over forty years' service at Peebles Hydro. Starting with the Army Catering Corps, he then worked with British Transport Hotels. But if cooking has been your life from the age of 15 it's very difficult to leave it completely. He still comes in three days a week to help out in the kitchen, particularly if there's a big event on:

"We like to promote the provenance of locally produced food strongly on our menus. That's an aspect that I enjoyed at events such as the Royal Highland Show in Edinburgh, where I would be part of the Borders Region stand and demonstrating what could be done with local produce. One year I had the privilege to show how I prepared 'Trout Balmoral' to Her Majesty the Queen."

Grand hotel - echoes of another age

The Peebles Hydro has for over a century been the iconic gathering place on a hillside above the town. Linger awhile in the hotel's hallway and terraces and you soon become aware of the sights and sounds of reunion: memories rekindled of a wedding in days long past, anticipation of a new marriage, the start of a new adventure and a time packed with celebration. Colleagues in business who have shaken off the hurly-burly of the office or a relentless life on the motorway, and are enlightening themselves on their missions in life. Or maybe just a simple, summer break where everyone, no matter what age or generation, can relax, alone, or together.

above:

Aqua aerobics in the Peebles Hydro Leisure Centre.

above, and opposite: The Team Spirit at Peebles Hydro.

It's easy to overlook the diminutive but no less characterful Park Hotel just a short distance away. Coming into the McMillan fold at the same time as the Hydro in 2004 and closer to the town, it possesses a quiet intimacy that draws a steady flow of guests, some of them regulars from the Hydro, but a great many coming here to be closer to Peebles' diverse shopping and activities. In a similar vein to the Fernhill Hotel at Portpatrick, the small team here is very hands-on in outlook. Val Carrick, who is Head Receptionist, appreciates the great variety of interest that multitasking brings to working here:

"We don't just do reception - we help other departments as well - waiting in the restaurant may be required - it gives you a bigger understanding into how the place runs. I have two other girls who are currently training in a job where personality is crucial. It's the first thing that guests will notice when they arrive: the welcome, the smile and the interest that's shown in them. You soon get feedback from guests about how they've been welcomed. That makes me feel good - because you know that their training is paying off."

The Park Hotel, Peebles

Julie Smith, General Manager
and the team at the Park Hotel.

Head Chef Jenny Thomson decided at the age of fifteen to embark on a career in the kitchen. After training in Dumfries, becoming Best Student in the process, she found work as a commis chef at the Hydro. After raising a family, she returned to work part-time at the Park:

"My mum was a keen baker – I'm from a farming background – and every Friday was baking day. I lived quite a few miles out of Moffat, so it wasn't a case of I'll just pop to the shops. Everything was made at home and food economy – making sure everything was used and not wasted – was very important."

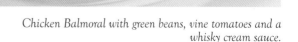

Chicken Balmoral with green beans, vine tomatoes and a whisky cream sauce.

A few of the many faces at the North West Castle Staff Reunion

11 - Awards, Accolades & Achievement

Friday, 6th July 2012: as the evening approaches there's more than the usual buzz of activity at the North West Castle Hotel. Alongside the influx of weekend visitors who are looking forward to a relaxing break, groups of people of all ages are arriving. Many are clutching envelopes and photographs. There are welcoming handshakes, hugs and kisses among friends who all share a common, very special bond: at some time or other during the past half-century, they have all worked for Hammy & Janet McMillan.

The best welcome of all comes from Hammy & Janet who, with their five children, all share their delight at meeting more than a hundred past employees. Many of them live in and around Stranraer, but quite a few have journeyed from much further afield. This evening of reunion is a unique opportunity to share memories, as well as reflect on the considerable achievements of the family. Housekeepers, receptionists, kitchen, dining room and maintenance staff: all are excitedly exchanging news and recalling good times as well as challenging times with the family.

Douglas McDavid, whose career began with the McMillans, regales all present with many of the stories he has already related for this book, and he reminds everybody of one outstanding fact: ever since North West Castle opened its doors in April 1962 the hotel has never closed; even for one day.

The pursuit of excellence is at the very heart of the business – not just in North West Castle, but throughout all six sister enterprises. The strong sense of 'family' can be found in every one of them, but at the same time it is subtly different. While big hotel chains need thick layers of corporate gloss, the McMillan family identity outshines all that.

The high regard in which the business is held, and in particular Hammy and Janet's unswerving commitment to guests and staff, has long been recognised within the industry and by those whose job it is to judge, comment and criticise. Winning your first award is always a memorable affair – but of course it doesn't end there. With that achievement there is the spur to do even better, to raise the game.

The list of awards that have been bestowed on the McMillans is reminiscent of the end credits for a Hollywood blockbuster. Back in the early sixties it was a case of ensuring that North West Castle measured up to the standards of the annual and unannounced gaze of AA & RAC inspectors. A three or four-starred listing in their authoritative annual handbooks, or a familiar yellow or blue badge on public display gave the traveller an idea of what to expect. Tourism agencies introduced their own standards and gradings, and the arrival of independent and occasionally outspoken critics such as Raymond Postgate (who founded the Good Food Guide), and Egon Ronay brought a new vibrancy to Britain's hospitality industry. The wider media - press, radio and television and the internet have all added to the momentum of increasing interest.

Staying ahead of these challenges ranks highly with the McMillans, whether it's through the guest questionnaires placed in the bedroom, or the preferred, more personal touch where hotel staff talk informally with the guests about their stay, and can then act quickly on their feedback.

A few of the many awards which have been presented to the McMillan family over the past fifty years.

Perhaps the McMillan philosophy is best summed up by Cally Palace's General Manager, Bob McWhir:

"You don't ask the staff for anything beyond their job – but every one of them will go the extra mile. Sometimes guests might have forgotten a small piece of kit – a phone charger, a camera card reader. We're usually able to help them out from our own resources. We keep a little history of our guests and their particular likes or dislikes – it might be a special tea for the bedroom, or duvets instead of blankets. Some guests like Melba toast – and that is also flagged up so that they get it at their dinner table instead of home-baked bread. Maybe a cushion on their chair; or a carver chair with arms, or peaches for breakfast. I almost regard the restaurant as a kind of home for the family – I make sure I know who's sitting where, remembering their name is all-important, especially if they've come back to the hotel. I remember serving some young kids when I was a schoolboy of 15. Now those kids have grown up, and are fully fledged lawyers or doctors. One of our regular guests knows every single member of staff by name, even their partner's name, where they live, and all about their grannies, cousins, second aunties. He even gets me to drive him around on a few occasions! It's amazing how some guests notice even the slightest change – you would be surprised at the feedback we got when we changed the typeface of our dinner menus!"

Attention to the tiniest detail - that's how the McMillan reputation has been made.

And reputation is the most precious asset of all.

Celebrating 50 years of service

1962 - 2012

McMillan
HOTELS

Janet and Hammy (the 'Mrs' and the 'Boss'), receive the Gold Laurel for Outstanding Achievement on the occasion of the Golden Jubilee of McMillan Hotels.

Acknowledgments and References

Photography: Except where indicated below, all photographs are
© Graham Riddell Photography, Innerleithen, EH44 6QQ.

Additional Photography: p15, 17, 64-65 (lower), 70, 76, 82, 90 (upper left), 94,
96, 97, 98, 100, 101, 104, 106, 107, 109, 113, 120, 127, 135 by Michael Marshall.

Aerial photograph of Glenapp Castle on p113 courtesy of Dr J. Palmer.

Archival photographs and other illustrative items have been largely drawn from
the McMillan family and individual hotel collections. Thanks must also go to
past and present members of staff who have also loaned material for the archival
project.

Historic postcards and philatelic items are from the author's collection.

Chapter 2, p15: Portrait of Rear Admiral Sir John Ross is reproduced by
permission of the National Galleries of Scotland

Chapter 10, p125: 'The Story of Peebles Hydro', by Heather Thom, 1987

    p127: 'A Nurse's War', by Brenda McBryde, Chatto & Windus 1979

Special thanks are due to the Stranraer Free Press for their assistance in providing
access to archival material.

Book design and layout by Breathing Space Productions, Isle of Whithorn,
Wigtownshire DG8 8JD

Printed by the Commercial Print division of
Stranraer & Wigtownshire Free Press, St Andrew Street, Stranraer DG9 7EB

Index

About the Author

Michael Marshall's professional career in broadcasting, film-making and photography spans almost fifty years. He trained with the BBC in London and then progressed to the television Farming Unit in Birmingham before moving north to set up a television documentary department for BBC Scotland in Aberdeen. He was responsible for the creation of *The Beechgrove Garden*, and the television version of *The Food Programme* with the acclaimed food writer Derek Cooper, before it transferred to BBC Radio 4. In 1978 he set up his own independent film and television production company Cinécosse, specialising in food, agriculture and tourism productions, and most notably the long-running award-winning series for Scottish Television, *Scotland's Larder*. This work brought him into close contact with the hospitality industry, working alongside many of the country's leading ambassadors and creative culinary and writing talents. Now living in south-west Scotland with his Dumfries-born wife Jean, he continues to pursue his professional interests in the media, as well as writing and passing on skills in digital techniques to folks of a similar vintage to himself.